WRITTEN SKILLS FOR SQE2

QUESTIONS & ANSWERS IN

WILLS AND THE ADMINISTRATION OF ESTATES

Elliot Schatzberger

Series editors: Amy and David Sixsmith

REVISE SQE

First published in 2026 by Fink Publishing Ltd

Impression number 10 9 8 7 6 5 4 3 2 1

British Library Cataloguing in Publication Data
A catalogue record for this book is available from the British Library
ISBN: 9781917183048

This book is also available in various ebook formats.
Ebook ISBN: 9781917183055

Cover and text design by BMLD (bmld.uk)
Production and typesetting by Westchester Publishing Services UK
Development editing by Llinos Edwards

Fink Publishing Ltd
E-mail: hello@revise4law.co.uk
www.revise4law.co.uk

Acknowledgements

The author and publisher would like to thank the following copyright holders for their kind permission to reproduce material in this book:
Bloomsbury Publishing, p. 27, extract from 'English Commorientes and Joint Tenancies - A Fresh Look at Section 184 of the Law of Property Act 1925' (2019). Hamed Ovaisi at SO Legal, p. 55, 'Wills and Undue Influence: Lessons from Rea v Rea' (2024). Owen Curry at XXIV Old Buildings, p. 48, 'Secret Trusts: Certainty of Intention and the Creation of Secret Trusts in a Recent Case' (March 2021). RELX (UK) Limited, trading as LexisNexis: *Halsbury's Laws of England*, pp. 50 and 51. Extracts from the SRA website in this book are owned by and published under licence from the Solicitors Regulation Authority of The Cube, 199 Wharfside Street, Birmingham, B1 1RN, which asserts its right to be identified as the author of this work in accordance with the Copyright, Designs and Patents Act 1988 Sections 77 and 78: www.sra.org.uk/solicitors/standards-regulations/financial-services-conduct-business-rules/. Please refer to the SRA website to ensure you are relying upon the correct version and most up to date version of the Standards.
Every effort has been made to obtain necessary permission with reference to copyright material. The publishers apologise if inadvertently any sources remain unacknowledged and will gladly make suitable arrangements with any copyright holders whom it has not been possible to contact.

Notes from the publisher

1. This book reflects the SQE2 assessment specification (updated May 2026), applicable for assessments from 1 September 2026.
2. While Fink Publishing has made every attempt to ensure that advice on the qualification and its assessment is accurate, the official specification and associated assessment guidance materials are the only authoritative source of information and should always be referred to for definitive guidance. See the SRA website at https://sqe.sra.org.uk. Note that the SRA may amend their assessment guidance (including the contents of the assessment specifications) at any point.
3. Fink Publishing has robust editorial processes to ensure the accuracy of the content in this publication, and every effort is made to ensure this publication is free of errors. We are, however, only human, and occasionally errors do occur. Fink Publishing is not liable for any misunderstandings that arise as a result of errors in this publication, but it is our priority to ensure that the content is accurate. If you spot an error, please do contact us at **revise4law.co.uk** so we can make sure it is corrected.

Contents

Contributors

THE AUTHOR

Dr Elliot Schatzberger is a qualified lawyer and has worked extensively in both criminal and civil law. He was called to the Bar of England and Wales in 2005. Elliot has been a legal educator for 20 years, teaching LLB, GDL and other postgraduate programmes at Middlesex University, City St George's University of London, Bayes Business School and the Open University. His doctorate was awarded in 2018 with a thesis on legal education. For the last decade Elliot has provided training for OSCE/QLTS delegates from around the globe. He also prepares students and overseas legal practitioners for the SQE examinations, in which his students and delegates have achieved an 80% pass rate to date.

Elliot is the co-narrator of *Revise SQE* Audiobooks.

SERIES EDITORS

Dr Amy Sixsmith is associate professor in law at the University of Sunderland and a senior fellow of Advance HE.

Dr David Sixsmith is assistant professor in law at Northumbria Law School and a senior fellow of Advance HE.

Introduction

Welcome to *Revise SQE: Legal Skills for SQE2*! This series of revision guides is designed to support you through the second element of your Solicitors Qualifying Examination, in which you will be tested on your ability to put the legal knowledge you acquired for your SQE1 assessment into six different practical contexts.

The key to successfully navigating your SQE2 assessment can be split into three distinct areas:

- understanding how you are being assessed and what you are being assessed on
- practising example scenarios
- comparing and contrasting your answers with sample answers.

Our SQE2 guides are here to help you with this process, providing you not only with helpful guidance and top tips for approaching all of the relevant skills but also with multiple sample questions for each assessable skill in each of the relevant legal disciplines. Samples of high- and lower-scoring threshold answers to each question are provided, to guide you in good practice and steer you away from potential pitfalls.

Using this series in conjunction with our series of SQE1 revision guides for SQE1, to ensure that your legal knowledge is accurate and up to date, will enable you to tackle your SQE2 assessment with confidence.

PREPARING YOURSELF FOR SQE

The SQE is the route to qualification for aspiring solicitors and consists of two parts, as shown in this table.

Assessment	Contents of assessment
SQE1	• 340 multiple-choice questions • Closed book • Assessed over 2 sittings • Over 10 hours in total
SQE2	• Practical legal skills • 16 written and oral assessments • Assesses 6 practical legal skills • Over 14 hours in total

In addition to the above assessments, all candidates will have to undertake two years' qualifying work experience. More information on the SQE assessments can be found on the SRA website.

It is important to note that the SQE can be perceived to be a 'harder' set of assessments than the Legal Practice Course (LPC). The reason for this, explained by the SRA, is that the LPC is designed to prepare candidates for 'day one' of their training contract; the SQE, on the other hand, is designed to prepare candidates for 'day one' of being a newly qualified solicitor. With that in mind, and a different style of assessments in place, it is understandable that you might feel nervous or wary of the SQE.

This revision guide series will focus on preparation for SQE2. The SQE2 assessment is challenging as it asks candidates to put into practice the knowledge that they acquired for SQE1. This style of assessment is likely to be different from what you will have experienced before. We hope to alleviate some of those concerns, with guidance on preparing for the SQE assessment, tips on how to approach the skills-based assessments and detailed commentaries on sample answers to aid your revision.

WHAT DOES SQE2 ENTAIL?

SQE2 is split into two parts: oral and written. The table below shows the contexts in which these skills are assessed.

Part	Skills	Contexts
Oral	Client interview and attendance note/ legal analysis (hereafter referred to as 'interviewing')	Property practice Wills and intestacy, probate administration and practice
	Advocacy	Dispute resolution Criminal litigation
Written	Case and matter analysis Legal research Legal writing Legal drafting	Criminal litigation Dispute resolution Property practice Wills and intestacy, probate administration and practice Business organisations, rules and procedures

Oral skills

You will sit four oral skills examinations, which will take place over two half-days.

On day one you will be assessed in:
- advocacy in the context of dispute resolution
- interviewing in the context of property practice.

On day two you will be assessed in:
- advocacy in the context of criminal litigation
- interviewing in the context of wills and intestacy, probate administration and practice.

Written skills

For the written skills assessment, you will sit 12 examinations, which will take place over three half-days. Every day you will be required to take an assessment in *each* of the written skills - case and matter analysis, legal research, legal writing and legal drafting.

On day one you will sit:
- two assessments in dispute resolution
- two assessments in criminal litigation.

On day two you will sit:

- two assessments in property practice
- two assessments in wills and intestacy, probate administration and practice.

On day three you will sit all four assessments in business organisations, rules and procedures.

HOW IS SQE2 MARKED?

Each of the SQE2 skills has its own set of assessment criteria. The *Revise SQE: Legal Skills for SQE2* series provides the following guidance:

- Oral skills – the criteria are outlined in ***Oral Skills for SQE2: Questions & Answers in Advocacy*** and examined in more depth in ***Oral Skills for SQE2: Client Interviewing and Negotiation*** and ***Oral Skills for SQE2: Advocacy***.
- Written skills – the criteria are outlined at the beginning of each chapter in our books covering the written skills for different legal contexts (see pages 2, 25, 65 and 84 in this text). The criteria are also explored in more detail in ***Introduction to Written Legal Skills for SQE2***.

The assessment is marked against the relevant criteria using the following scale:

A. Superior performance: well above the competency requirements of the assessment.
B. Clearly satisfactory: clearly meets the competency requirements of the assessment.
C. Marginal pass: on balance, just meets the competency requirements of the assessment.
D. Marginal fail: on balance, just fails to meet the competency requirements of the assessment.
E. Clearly unsatisfactory: clearly does not meet the competency requirements of the assessment.
F. Poor performance: well below the competency requirements of the assessment.

Your mark will be calculated by converting the grade into a numerical mark, with A representing 5 marks and F representing 0 marks.

The scaled scoring system

The SRA uses a scaled scoring system for all SQE2 assessments. This approach is designed to ensure that candidate scores are comparable across different assessment sittings, thereby providing a fair and consistent measure of candidate performance. The same system is in place for all SQE1 assessments.

The scaled scoring system works in the following way:

- Initially, candidates will receive a 'raw score' based on their performance across the 16 assessment stations in SQE2.
- A pass mark is then set for each assessment window. The pass mark is determined using statistical methods that account for any differences in question difficulty. This ensures fairness across different exam versions.
- Candidate raw scores are then converted to a common scale ranging from 0 to 500, with the pass mark consistently set at 300. This standardisation allows for direct comparisons between candidates' performances, regardless of the specific assessments they completed.

When you access your results, you will be able to see:

- a detailed breakdown of your results by assessment station (results will be expressed as marks from 0 to 5 for each assessment criterion across each of the 16 assessment stations)
- your overall mark expressed as a percentage
- your scaled score out of 500 - remember that the pass mark will always be set at 300.

For more information about the scaled scoring system, visit the SRA website.

It is very important that you are aware of the standard you are required to meet. The competence standard is that of a Day One Solicitor, which is mapped against Level 3 of the Threshold Standard for the Statement of Solicitor Competence. This is available on the SRA website, and we would encourage you to review this prior to sitting your SQE2 assessment.

The assessors

In terms of who will be assessing you against this standard and the relevant skills criteria, the interview will be marked by the person you are interviewing, whilst the remaining assessments (attendance note, advocacy and all written skills) will be marked by a solicitor. All assessors will have received training on how to assess a candidate's performance against the relevant criteria. It is therefore essential that you tackle your assessments in the same way that you would if you were a fully qualified solicitor on the first day of practice, ie with professionalism, confidence and calmness. This will come across to the assessors in the examination itself: remember that they are fundamentally assessing your suitability for practice!

WHERE DOES *REVISE SQE* COME INTO IT?

This new series of revision guides for SQE2 will provide you with helpful tips and advice on how to tackle each skill assessment in the relevant contexts. Each book provides a range of example threshold answers to SQE2-style assessment questions, which you can use to practise and assess your answers against, to see how you are performing in each individual area. This is designed to assist with your revision and consolidate your understanding of how key topics could be assessed in the SQE2 examinations. We hope that this series will give clarity for assessment focus, provide useful tips for sitting SQE2 and act as a general revision aid.

Finally, always keep in mind that, whilst SQE2 is primarily a skills-based assessment, you are still being tested on your knowledge of the law. It is therefore important that you conduct an honest self-evaluation on the areas of the SQE1 specification with which you feel you need further support. *Revise SQE* can help you with this:

- Check out the 'SQE1 Revision Checklist' for each of our SQE1 revision guides on our website: **www.revise4law.co.uk**. These will help you to identify which substantive topics you feel confident about being assessed on, and which ones you need to revise.
- All of our *Revise SQE* revision guides are mapped to the relevant SRA specifications for SQE1. Before taking the SQE2 assessments, remember to look back at our revision guides for SQE1 if you have any gaps in your legal knowledge.

1

Case and matter analysis

MAKE SURE YOU KNOW

This chapter covers the skill of case and matter analysis in the context of wills and the administration of estates (referred to from this point as 'wills'). Case and matter analysis in wills is one of the legal skills that may be assessed on day two of the SQE2 assessments; see the Introduction for more detail. Mastering the skill of effective case analysis is key to success in other written skills assessments too, especially writing and drafting, and also the oral skills assessments of advocacy and client interviewing. You will need to develop the ability to analyse a scenario and apply the correct law and procedure to the facts of the case.

Bear in mind that the SQE2 assessment can test your knowledge not only of the processes associated with wills but also of the application of relevant legal principles to those processes. Before attempting the questions in this chapter, review the contents of ***Revise SQE: Wills and the Administration of Estates***, ***Revise SQE: Land Law***, ***Revise SQE: Trusts Law***, ***Revise SQE: Property Practice*** and ***Revise SQE: Business Law and Practice***.

This chapter provides examples of how different topics such as intestacy, inheritance tax and testamentary clauses could arise in the context of an SQE2 case and matter analysis assessment on wills.

SQE ASSESSMENT ADVICE

As you work through this chapter, remember to pay particular attention in your revision to:

- selecting relevant information about the legal issue or the client's problem from the material provided in your instructions, including any documents that are provided
- using your knowledge to substantiate/support your answer to the matter in question
- addressing relevant legal and/or commercial considerations and focusing on the client's priorities, objectives and constraints
- using understandable and simple language to convey facts and information effectively so that the client comprehends how the law applies to their case
- using correct legal terminology, identifying the relevant legal principles and applying them correctly to the facts of the client's case
- ensuring your legal analysis is sufficiently detailed in the context of the case's facts
- where relevant, spotting ethical or professional conduct issues and advising how they might be addressed (ethical issues often arise when dealing with clients' wills).

See the Appendix for the SRA's performance indicators in case and matter analysis, and how to demonstrate your competency in this skill.

■ INTRODUCTION TO CASE AND MATTER ANALYSIS IN WILLS

The SQE2 assessment in case and matter analysis will contain a typical scenario from day-to-day legal practice when dealing with wills. When practising in this field, you need to develop the ability to consider the details of a case, analyse the facts to ascertain whether the matter can be resolved in the best interest of the client and then provide advice to the client. This can be especially difficult owing to the emotive nature of the topic and the potential sensitivity of such a client.

The case and matter analysis assessment will be based on a case study with documents. Your task will be to produce a written report for a partner that includes a legal analysis of the case and provides client-focused advice. This could include options and strategies for negotiation and will often involve issues of professional conduct and ethics. This chapter will provide examples of how to achieve this whilst meeting the assessment criteria for SQE2 case and matter analysis.

To create a logical and clear response to your SQE2 case and matter analysis assessment, approach the question in a structured manner. Try adopting the following method:

1. Once you have read all the documentation, write down the question(s) being asked of you.
2. Write down the key facts from the instructions that you feel are relevant to answering the question.
3. Check the information in your instructions carefully and then write down the key law or procedure that you think is relevant.
4. Check that the law identified in point 3 above relates back to and answers the question(s) you identified in point 1.
5. Structure your written report around those key facts and legal issues, using headings and subheadings.
6. Complete your written report.
7. Review your answer, keeping in mind the SQE2 case and matter analysis assessment criteria.

SQE2 case and matter analysis assessment criteria

Try to remember these points as you construct your response, and refer back to them as you review our sample answers in this chapter:

Skills

1. Identify relevant facts.
2. Provide client-focused advice (ie advice which demonstrates an understanding of the problem from the client's point of view and what the client wants to achieve, not just from a legal perspective).
3. Use clear, precise, concise and acceptable language.

Application of law

4. Apply the law correctly to the client's situation.
5. Apply the law comprehensively to the client's situation.
6. Identify any ethical and professional conduct issues and exercise judgement to resolve them honestly and with integrity.

Assessment technique

When reviewing your answer, check you have dealt with each relevant fact or legal issue. Cross-referencing the relevant information presented in the documents and case study will prevent you from omitting important details. Make sure that all facts and figures are accurate, especially if the question involves assets or inheritance tax.

For more detailed support and guidance on how to meet the SQE2 case and matter analysis assessment criteria, see ***Introduction to Written Legal Skills for SQE2***, chapter 1, Case and matter analysis.

In ***Revise SQE: Wills and the Administration of Estates***, we considered the rules relating to inheritance tax (chapter 10) and intestacy (chapter 5). Question 1 below demonstrates how your knowledge of inheritance tax could be tested in the context and format of an SQE2 case and matter analysis assessment.

■ QUESTION 1

Email to candidate

From: Partner
Sent: 13 June 202#
To: Candidate
Subject: Amram Mazzun (deceased)

Yesterday I spoke to a new client Shuhaib Mazzun (37), whose father, Amram, died suddenly last week. Amram is survived by his partner, Parveen, and their two children, Shuhaib and his sister, Sarai. Shuhaib was very distressed but managed to give me some key information in relation to his late father's will and assets, which is accurate as far as we know:

Shuhaib is aware that his father left a valid will when he died (**Attachment 1**). I have also attached the Joint Ownership form (**Attachment 2**) as Amram owned a property with Parveen.

Sarai (27) got married four years ago, and on the occasion of her wedding Amram made a gift of £75,000 to his daughter. He did not make any other gifts or transfers in the last seven years of his life. It is noted that neither the Transferable Nil Rate Band (TNRB) nor the Residence Nil Rate Band (RNRB) applies to Amram's estate.

In his will, Amram left £10,000 to the Conservation Trust (a registered charity). The remainder of his estate is to be shared between his partner, Parveen (neither of them was ever married), Shuhaib and Sarai.

Assets

Amram owned the following assets in his sole name unless stated otherwise:

1. Santander bank account, including interest at the date of death: balance £155,600.
2. Work bonus payment due at date of death: amount owed £500.
3. Shares in Booker PLC, which has no connection with Amram: valued at £570,000.
4. Life assurance policy written in trust for Shuhaib and Sarai: lump sum of £150,000 to share.
5. A second-hand Renault car (Amram's main mode of transport): value £5,000.
6. A terraced property at 15 Longbourn Road: value £350,000.

At the date of death Amram had debts of £4,325, and initial funeral expenses of £1,600 have been incurred.

Advice and analysis required
Shuhaib would like advice on the inheritance tax that might be payable on his late father's estate. Shuhaib wonders whether a large amount may be owed and is concerned about this as he is not in a stable financial position.

Please provide advice and analysis for me to use as the basis of a letter to the client. In providing your advice, bear in mind that Shuhaib is not a lawyer. The client would like brief explanations of the relevant principles of inheritance tax where appropriate, so please include these in your advice and analysis. Do not include advice about the procedure at this stage, including how payments are made and by whom.

Please set out your advice and analysis on the following:

1. **What is Amram's cumulative total at the date of his death?**
2. **How will the cumulative total impact on the calculation of inheritance tax for his death estate?**
3. **What inheritance tax will be payable on Amram's death? Remember, you are not required to consider the TNRB or RNRB.**

Thanks

Partner

Attachments:

1. Amram Mazzun's will
2. Joint Ownership form

Attachment 1

Will of Amram Mazzun

I AMRAM MAZZUN of 15 Longbourn Road, Wimbledon LONDON SW19 4ZC **HEREBY REVOKE** all former wills and testamentary dispositions made by me **AND DECLARE** this to be my last will and testament

1. **I APPOINT** my solicitors **SIMONE JONES AND LISA EDWARDS** of Bradmans Law LLP (hereinafter called 'my Trustees' which expression shall include the trustees or trustee for the time being) to be the executors and trustees of my will
2. **I GIVE** to my partner **PARVEEN SHAH** any shares I may have at the date of my death in Booker PLC absolutely
3. **I GIVE** to my best friend **IMRAN ZOYA** any motor vehicle I own at my death absolutely and free of tax and costs of transfer

4.1. **I GIVE** to **THE CONSERVATION TRUST** (Registered Charity No. 12348765) the sum of **TEN THOUSAND POUNDS** (£10,000) absolutely and free of tax

4.2. **THE** receipt of the person who appears to be a proper officer of each charity shall be a sufficient discharge to my Trustees

4.3. **IF** at the date of my death any named charity has amalgamated with another charity or has changed its name the gift to it shall not fail but shall take effect as a gift to the body in its new form

4.4. **IF** at the date of my death any named charitable organisation has not amalgamated with another charity or changed its name but has otherwise ceased to exist or ceased to be a registered charity my Trustees shall pay the legacy to the charitable organisation which they in their absolute discretion shall consider most nearly to fulfil the charitable objects which they believe I intended to benefit

5. **I GIVE** to my daughter **SARAI MAZZUN** of 4 Queen Street, Hammersmith, London the sum of **FIVE HUNDRED POUNDS** (£500) absolutely and free of tax, to be paid from any outstanding work bonus owed to me at the time of my death

6.1. **I GIVE** to my Executors and Trustees all my real and personal property not hereby nor by any Codicil hereto otherwise disposed of whatsoever and wheresoever (including any property over which I may have a general power of appointment or disposition by Will) (hereafter referred to as 'my Residuary Estate')

6.2. My Executors and Trustees shall pay out of my Residuary Estate my debts, funeral and testamentary expenses and legacies and all inheritance tax

6.3. I give my Residuary Estate to my Trustees to hold on trust for such of my partner **PARVEEN SHAH** and my two children, **SHUHAIB MAZZUN** and **SARAI MAZZUN**, if more than one in equal shares and for their own use and benefit absolutely

6.4. If all of the said **PARVEEN SHAH**, **SHUHAIB MAZZUN** and **SARAI MAZZUN** shall die before me, I give my Residuary Estate to my Trustees to distribute to any charity specialising in conservation as they see fit

7. **I DESIRE** that my body be buried at the family plot at Wimbledon Cemetery London SW19
8. The Standard Provisions and all the Special Provisions of the Society of Trust and Estate Practitioners (2nd Edition) shall apply

IN WITNESS whereof I have hereunto set my hand this 14th day of June 2020

SIGNED BY the above named AMRAM MAZZUN in our joint presence and then by us in his	Amram Mazzun

Danyal Nauroz

Danyal Nauroz
2 The Village
Wimbledon

Muna Ben Bakhsh

Muna Ben Bakhsh
144 Tooting High Street
London

Attachment 2

HM Land Registry
Trust Information

JO

Any parts of the form that are not typed should be completed in black ink and in block capitals.

This form may accompany an application in Form AP1, FR1 or ADV1 where:

- panel 9 of Form FR1 or ADV1 has not been completed and the applicant is more than one person, or
- the Form AP1 relates to a transfer (in Form AS1, AS3, TP1, TP2, TR1, TR2 or TR5) or a prescribed clauses lease (within rule 58A of the Land Registration Rules 2003) of a registered estate to more than one person (the Joint Owners), and
  - the declaration of trust panel in the transfer or lease has not been completed and/or the transfer has not been executed by the Joint Owners, and
  - the estate transferred or leased is not a rent charge, franchise, profit or manor.

For information on how HM Land Registry processes your personal information, see our Personal Information Charter.

Enter the same information as either in the transfer or lease to the Joint Owners or in panel 6 of Form ADV1. Leave blank if this form accompanies a Form FR1.	1	Title number(s) of the property: KZ437982
Insert address including postcode (if any) or other description of the property as it appears either in the transfer or lease to the Joint Owners, in panel 3 of Form ADV1 or in panel 2 of Form FR1.	2	Property: 15, Longbourn Road, Wimbledon, London SW19 4ZC
	3	Date: 19 November 2010
Give full name(s) and address(es), as in either the transfer or lease to the Joint Owners, panels 6 and 7 of Forms ADV1 or panels 6 and 8 of Form FR1.	4	Joint Owners: AMRAM MAZZUN and PARVEEN SHAH [currently of 266a Badon Road Wimbledon SW19 4ZZ]

Complete either this or panel 6. Place an 'X' in the appropriate box. If completing the fourth box, insert details either of the trust or of the trust instrument under which the Joint Owners hold the property. The registrar will enter a Form A restriction in the register if an 'X' is placed: – in the second or third box, or – in the fourth box, unless it is clear that the Joint Owners hold on trust for themselves alone as joint tenants. If this panel is completed, each Joint Owner must sign. Please refer to Joint property ownership and practice guide 24: private trusts of land for further guidance. These are both available on the GOV.UK website.	5 ☒ The Joint Owners declare that they are to hold the property on trust for themselves alone as joint tenants ☐ The Joint Owners declare that they are to hold the property on trust for themselves alone as tenants in common in equal shares ☐ The Joint Owners declare that they hold the property on trust for themselves alone as tenants in common in the following unequal shares: (*complete*) ☐ The Joint Owners are to hold the property (*complete*): Signature of each of the Joint Owners Amram Mazzun Parveen Shah Date: 19/11/2010
If this panel is completed, a conveyancer must sign.	6 Under the term of a written declaration of trust dated (*complete*) the Joint Owners ☐ hold the property on trust as joint tenants for themselves alone ☐ do not hold the property on trust as joint tenants for themselves alone Signature of conveyancer ________________ Date:

WARNING

If you dishonestly enter information or make a statement that you know is, or might be, untrue or misleading, and intend by doing so to make a gain for yourself or another person, or to cause loss or the risk of loss to another person, you may commit the offence of fraud under section 1 of the Fraud Act 2006, the maximum penalty for which is 10 years' imprisonment or an unlimited fine, or both.

Failure to complete this form with proper care may result in a loss of protection under the Land Registration Act 2002 if, as a result, a mistake is made in the register.

Under section 66 of the Land Registration Act 2002 most documents (including this form) kept by the registrar relating to an application to the registrar or referred to in the register are open to public inspection and copying. If you believe a document contains prejudicial information, you may apply for that part of the document to be made exempt using Form EX1, under rule 136 of the Land Registration Rules 2003.

* * *

■ YOUR TURN

Have a go at answering question 1, remembering the guidance on pages 1-3.

- Remember the structured approach in the SRA's assessment criteria on page 2.
- Create a list of the most salient legal issues raised by the question, especially the assets and their value.
- Consider the client's perspective at all times.
- Timings are important: you will need to prepare and write your answer in one hour.

SQE1 Functioning legal knowledge link

Remember from chapter 10 of ***Revise SQE: Wills and Administration of Estates*** that the rules of inheritance tax must be applied when a deceased leaves assets in an estate. You may also need to note from chapter 6 that any property held as joint tenants before death passes to a surviving joint tenant through survivorship, although there is still an impact on inheritance tax to consider, and from chapter 5 that certain assets, such as life assurance policies in trust, pass outside an estate.

EVALUATING YOUR ANSWER

When you have attempted question 1, mark it yourself against the SQE2 case and matter analysis assessment criteria. Do you think your attempt met the threshold standard?

Now compare your attempt with the following key legal points and two sample answers to question 1. A circled number indicates that commentary is provided for this part of the answer. The commentary explains whether or not the sample satisfies the assessment criteria, and accordingly whether it is likely to meet the SQE2 threshold standard.

➥Key legal points: question 1

The rules for inheritance tax are laid down in different provisions of the Inheritance Tax Act 1984. You will need to take the following steps in order to answer the question:

- Step 1: Identify the cumulative total. Remember that the effect of the cumulative total is to reduce the nil rate band available for his death estate.
  - The nil rate band is currently £325,000.
  - The cumulative total is the sum of the chargeable value of chargeable transfers made in the previous seven years.
- Steps 2 and 3: Identify and value the taxable estate.
- Step 4: Deduct debts.
- Step 5: Deduct any available exemptions and reliefs.
- Step 6: Calculate the inheritance tax.

As per your instructions, ignore TRNB and RNRB, and how or by whom payments are made.

■ SAMPLE ANSWER 1 TO QUESTION 1

Our new client is Shuhaib Mazzun (37) and we are assisting him in relation to the sudden death of his father, Amram, last week. Shuhaib is concerned about the amount of inheritance tax that is owed by his father's estate. We have received some information from Shuhaib that, as far as we know, is accurate, and documents including a copy of his father's will and also a Land Registry Joint Ownership document, as Amram owned a property (15 Longbourn Road) with his partner, Parveen.

Amram made a gift of £75,000 to his daughter, Sarai, four years ago on the occasion of her wedding (s 20 Inheritance Tax Act 1984 applies here). Before his death Amram had made no other lifetime transfers in the last seven years. Amram was not married so the Transferable NRB (TNRB) does not apply to Amram's estate, and, as he is not passing his primary residence to direct descendants, the Residence NRB (RNRB) does not apply either. ❶

1. Cumulative total ❷

We have been asked to provide detail as to Amram's cumulative total at the date of his death. My calculations below show that this amounts to **£64,000**:

The gift of £75,000 was given less than seven years before Amram's death, so inheritance tax will apply. However, there is an exemption of **£5,000** where the gift is given by a parent of one of the parties in consideration of a marriage. Two annual exemptions (AEs) of £3,000 are also allowed (s 19 Inheritance Tax Act 1984), so there is a maximum of 2 × AE (**£6,000**) that may be available if neither of the previous year's AEs was used. No other transfers have been made in the current year. **The cumulative total is therefore:**

£75,000 − £5,000 − (2 × £3,000) = £64,000 ❸

2. Effect of cumulative total on the estate

The effect of the cumulative total is to reduce the threshold for inheritance tax, called the nil rate band (NRB), available for Amram's death estate. The NRB is fixed at £325,000 but, when the cumulative total (£64,000) is subtracted from this, Amram's estate will therefore have an available NRB of **£261,000**.

Please note the following points:

1. The cumulative total is the sum of the chargeable value of transfers made in the previous seven years. The chargeable value of the failed £75,000 gift is now £64,000. ❹
2. Amram left a valid will that gives £10,000 to the Conservation Trust. This is a registered charity and therefore exempt, according to s 23 Inheritance Tax Act 1984.
3. The remainder of his estate is shared between his partner, Parveen (neither of them has ever been married), and his two adult children, Shuhaib and Sarai.
4. Amram owned the following assets in his sole name unless stated otherwise:
   a) Santander bank account, including interest at the date of death (balance £155,600).
   b) Work bonus payment due at date of death (amount owed £500).
   c) Shares in Booker PLC, which has no connection with Amram (worth £570,000).
   d) Life assurance policy written in trust for Shuhaib and Sarai (lump sum £150,000).
   e) A second-hand Renault car, Amram's main mode of transport (value £5,000).
   f) A terraced property at 15 Longbourn Road that was held as joint tenants with Parveen (total value £350,000). ❺

At the date of death Amram has debts of £4,325, and initial funeral expenses of £1,600 have been incurred. These need to be deducted from the estate first.

3. Tax payable on Amram's death

We can follow a number of steps to determine the amount of inheritance tax payable on Amram's death. Neither the TNRB nor the RNRB applies to this case. The amount of inheritance tax owed by Amram's estate is **£244,670**; see below for my calculations.

Step 1: Identify the cumulative total
Amram's cumulative total is **£64,000**. This has the effect of reducing his NRB to **£261,000** (£325,000 – £64,000).

Steps 2 and 3: Identify and value the taxable estate
The following items are included in the taxable estate:

Bank account	£155,600
Work bonus	£500
Shares	£570,000
Personal effects	£5,000
15 Longbourn Road	£157,500
TOTAL	**£888,600**

It is important to note that:

- The life assurance policy is not included in the taxable estate as this was written in trust.
- 15 Longbourn Road was valued at £157,500 as this is the deceased's half share, less 10% because he co-owned with someone who was not his spouse. Joint property is included however it is owned, regardless of whether it is held as joint tenants or tenants in common (HMRC Guidance). ❻

Step 4: Deduct debts
Amram had debts of £4,325, and funeral expenses of £1,600 have been incurred. Both of these items can be deducted from the taxable estate:

£888,600 – £5,925 = £882,675

Step 5: Deduct any available exemptions and reliefs
We are told that Amram left £10,000 by will to charity. This will qualify for 100% charity exemption, so this amount can also be deducted from the taxable estate:

£882,675 - £10,000 = £872,675

No business property relief is available, as, although Amram owned company shares in Booker PLC, there was no controlling interest. ❼

Step 6: Calculate inheritance tax
Apply available NRB: 0 to £261,000 @ 0% = 0 (see step 1 above)

£872,675 – £261,000 = £611,675

Above the NRB apply 40%:

£611,675 × 40% = £244,670

The amount of inheritance tax owed by Amram's estate is therefore **£244,670.** ❽

COMMENTARY

❶ This is an excellent start. The candidate has identified the key issue as inheritance tax and begun by explaining and applying relevant rules such as recognising lifetime transfers; they also illustrate what the instructions state is not to be discussed. There is also good statutory reference here to the Inheritance Tax Act 1984 so the assessment criteria are being met by applying law to the scenario. There is also excellent use of the materials such as Attachment 2, the Joint Ownership form: the candidate has spotted that the property was owned as joint tenants.

❷ The candidate has used numbered headings effectively to structure the report. This will help the partner to use this information in the letter to the client, and immediately shows the SQE2 assessor that all aspects of the question have been addressed.

❸ The candidate explains cumulative total in a way that a lay client could understand. The candidate also applies the facts effectively, dealing accurately with the wedding gift and the two AE allowances, setting out the correct figure for the cumulative total. They have included the statutory authority for the partner's benefit, but this could easily be removed for the client letter. This demonstrates the candidate's use of precise and acceptable language as required by the assessment criteria.

❹ The candidate has effectively explained both the cumulative total and the failed transfer, and helpfully provided a running total of how the cumulative total affects the nil rate band. The client should be in no doubt so far as to how this is beginning to be calculated.

❺ It is good practice to set out the key facts as given in instructions so the client can clearly see at a glance what the relevant assets are and how they may be included or ignored for the purposes of calculating inheritance tax. The candidate achieves this effectively and has noticed the significance of joint tenancy in the final asset listed here.

❻ The candidate has correctly omitted the assets that would not be included in an inheritance tax calculation: first, they have excluded the life assurance policy, and second they have expertly noticed that, although ownership of a joint tenancy property vests in the surviving joint tenant, inheritance tax is still to be paid on the half taken by the survivor, less a 10% discount as stated by HMRC to recognise the fact that the property was co-owned by non-spouses or civil partners. This response demonstrates client focus and the correct and comprehensive application of the law to the case, as required by the assessment criteria.

❼ The candidate has also effectively dealt with the charitable donation, which is a deductible allowance. They have also spotted that the shares are not subject to business property relief as they are non-controlling interest shares. This is a clear analysis of the client's information. The candidate also demonstrates good practice by giving a running total as they move through the different steps, so that the client will have a clear view of the calculations.

❽ Finally, the candidate accurately applies the 40% to the remaining balance over £261,000 and ends with the accurate amount. This is exactly what the client wishes to know, and the candidate has carefully addressed all three elements of the question.

Does this answer meet the threshold?

The sample answer contains all of the information relating to inheritance tax that the client requires and that the candidate has been asked to provide. It applies the relevant legislation and HMRC rules and then discusses *how* they apply to the client's circumstances in this scenario. The answer uses clear, succinct language and is legally correct. As a mathematical exercise, the correct figure for inheritance tax is given. This response is therefore likely to meet the threshold standard for SQE2 case and matter analysis.

Now consider the second sample answer to question 1.

■ SAMPLE ANSWER 2 TO QUESTION 1

Amram died a week ago but before he died he gave £75,000 to his daughter, Sarai, as a wedding gift. It appears there were no other gifts made in his lifetime. ❶

Cumulative total

Amram's cumulative total is £70,000. Amram had not made any other gifts so according to inheritance tax rules the gift of £75,000 given less than seven years before death fails in relation to the full £75,000. However, there is an exemption of **£5,000** where it is a gift given in consideration of a marriage if made by a parent of one of the parties, so the cumulative total is **£70,000.** ❷

Effect of the cumulative total

The effect of the cumulative total is to reduce the nil rate band available for his death estate. Amram will therefore have an available NRB of **£255,000** (£325,000 – £70,000).

It should be noted that the cumulative total is the sum of the chargeable value of chargeable transfers made in the previous seven years. The chargeable value of the failed transfer is £70,000. ❸

It is also noted that Amram died and left a valid will that gives £10,000 to the Conservation Trust (a registered charity), and the remainder of his estate is shared between his partner, Parveen (neither of them has ever been married), and their two adult children, Shuhaib and Sarai.

To clarify, Amram owned the following assets in his sole name unless stated otherwise:

- Santander bank account, including interest at the date of death
- Work bonus payment due at date of death
- Shares in Booker PLC, which has no connection with Amram
- Life assurance policy written in trust for Shuhaib and Sarai (lump)
- A second-hand Renault car (Amram's main mode of transport)
- A terraced property at 15 Longbourn Road held as joint tenants with Parveen.

At the date of death Amram had debts of £4,325 and funeral expenses of £1,600 have been incurred. ❹

Tax payable on Amram's death

Step 1: Identify the cumulative total
Amram's cumulative total is **£70,000**. This has the effect of reducing his NRB to **£255,000** (£325,000 – £70,000).

Steps 2 and 3: Identify and value the taxable estate
The following items are included in the taxable estate:

Bank accounts	£155,600
Work bonus	£500
Shares	£570,000
Personal effects	£5,000
15 Longbourn Road	£175,000
TOTAL:	**£906,100**

Note that the life assurance policy was not included above as this was written in trust, and 15 Longbourn Road was valued at £175,000 as this is the deceased's half share. Joint property is included however it is owned. ❺

Step 4: Deduct debts
Amram had debts of £4,325 and additional funeral expenses of £1,600 have been incurred. Both of these items can be deducted, to leave **£900,175** (£906,100 – £4,325 – £1,600).

Step 5: Deduct any available exemptions and reliefs
We are told that Amram left £10,000 by will to charity and this will qualify for 100% charity exemption. We must therefore deduct £10,000 from £900,175, to give a taxable value of **£890,175.** ❻

Step 6: Calculate the inheritance tax
Apply available NRB: 0 to £255,000 @ 0% = 0 (see step 1 above)
Above the NRB apply 40%: £890,175 – £255,000 @ 40% = (£635,175×40%) to pay. **£254,070 IHT** ❼

Thanks

Candidate

COMMENTARY

❶ This is a rather vague start. Although the candidate has identified that the gift to Sharai affects inheritance tax, the opening paragraph is imprecise as to timing and also does not set out the fact that TNRB and RNRB are to be excluded. There is also no reference here to the Inheritance Tax Act 1984, so the candidate is not signposting to the assessor that they are applying the correct law to the scenario, as required by the assessment criteria. There is an error: gifts in 'his lifetime' are not relevant, only transfers in the last seven years. Furthermore, there is no reference to the joint tenancy identified in the instructions and the Joint Ownership form.

❷ The candidate begins to explain correctly what cumulative total means, but not in a way that a lay client could easily understand: 'fails in relation to the full £75,000' would need further explanation. Remember that your use of language must be clear, precise, concise and acceptable to meet the assessment criteria. The candidate then fails to apply the facts effectively: they deal accurately with the wedding gift but miss the two AE allowances, so that they arrive at the wrong figure for the cumulative total. This means that all calculations that follow will be inaccurate, so this is a fatal error.

❸ The candidate has effectively explained the cumulative total but, as seen in point 2, they have failed to give an accurate running total of how the cumulative total affects the NRB. The client will now be wrongly informed. The candidate continues to omit statutory references, which gives the impression that the answer lacks authority.

❹ Although it can be good practice to set out the key facts as given in instructions so the client can quickly see the relevant assets and gauge how they may be included or ignored for calculating inheritance tax, it is not useful to set these out without their values as the candidate has done here.

❺ The candidate correctly sets down the asset of the life assurance policy as not included in an inheritance tax calculation. However, although the candidate has noticed that ownership of a joint tenancy property vests in the surviving joint tenant, and that inheritance tax is still to be paid on the half taken by the survivor, they miss the 10% discount as stated by HMRC (the reference to this authority is missed too) to recognise the fact that the property was co-owned by non-spouses or civil partners, as is the case here. Because this discount is not applied, there are further inaccuracies in the mathematics.

❻ The candidate has effectively dealt with deducting debts and the charitable donation being a deductible allowance, but they have not explained, as was done in sample answer 1, why the full value of the shares is included (no business property relief applicable). The running total remains incorrect.

❼ Finally, the candidate has applied the 40% to the inaccurate NRB of £255,000 and so ends with an incorrect amount of inheritance tax. The client now believes that they are to pay £9,400 more tax than is required, and could make a formal complaint against a solicitor based on this kind of negligence. The report also finished hurriedly, with no clear statement of the actual inheritance tax to be paid. Note how the calculations in sample answer 2 are not set out as clearly as in sample answer 1. Make it easy for your assessor to work through your calculations by laying out your figures and equations clearly, using new lines for better clarity and precision where required.

Does this answer meet the threshold?

When assessing the second report against the SQE2 case and matter analysis assessment criteria, it is unlikely that it would meet the threshold standard. The candidate has misinterpreted the law and mathematics, and made errors in relation to allowances and co-owned property, which will mislead the client. The answer was also a little brief and does not show full understanding of how inheritance tax is calculated.

The SQE2 assessment can focus on any of the areas on the SQE1 wills specification. Below is another example of how a different part of the specification - intestacy - could arise in the context of an SQE2 case and matter analysis assessment.

■ QUESTION 2

Email to candidate

From: Partner
Sent: 13 June 202#
To: Candidate
Subject: Vito Andolini (deceased)

We have recently been instructed by Carmela Andolini. I spoke to Carmela yesterday and she would like advice regarding the estate of her late husband, Vito, who died intestate last month. Vito was a successful businessman who owned a number of assets at the time of his death, including properties and cars.

Vito had a relatively large family. He was married to Carmela at the time of his death and is survived by his mother, Maria. Vito and Carmela's eldest child, Sonny, is deceased but had been married to Sandra and they had a child, Frank (six years old). Vito and Carmela's second child, Vincent, was adopted and is married to Mila. They have a child, Santino (two years old). Connie is Vito and Carmela's third child, who is 18 years old and married to Carlo.

Vito held the following assets in his sole name unless otherwise stated:

1. Apartment in Little Venice, London (value £1.5 million) and contents (value £80,000), both owned with Carmela as beneficial joint tenants.
2. Country house in Wimbledon, London (value £350,000).
3. Contents of Wimbledon house (value £100,000), owned with Carmela as beneficial joint tenants.
4. Two 4×4 Land Rover cars and one motorbike (value £28,000).
5. Nationwide Building Society current account (balance £1,600).
6. NatWest savings account (balance £18,000), in joint names with Carmela.
7. Quoted (non-controlled) shares (value £575,000).
8. Audi convertible sports car (value £4,800).
9. Personal possessions (value £1,200).
10. Unpaid salary owed to Vito (£1,200).
11. Life assurance policy with Insure4U (policy proceeds £50,000). Written in trust for Frank.

Vito's funeral expenses total £1,800. He is to be buried at Wimbledon Cemetery in accordance with wishes he has already expressed in previous instructions.

I have been informed by Carmela that there are no debts. You are not required to deal with inheritance tax and estate administration expenses other than the funeral expenses.

I have attached an email received from Vito's son Vincent this morning (Attachment 1) and an extract of the statutory provisions on statutory trusts at s 47 Administration of Estates Act 1925 (Attachment 2) to assist you.

Please set out your advice and analysis on the following:

1. **What assets fall within Vito's succession estate? What is the value of his net succession estate available for distribution?**
2. **Who will inherit Vito's assets? What amount/property will each beneficiary receive?**
3. **Should the painting referred to in Attachment 1 be categorised as a personal belonging? Advise the client on how this asset affects the estate.**

Thanks

Partner

Attachment 1

From: Vincent Andolini
Sent: 13 June 202#
To: Partner
Subject: Painting

Hello,

You are being instructed by my mother, Carmela Andolini, regarding the estate of my father, Vito, who died intestate last week.

We have just remembered that my father owned a fabulous Modigliani painting that is extremely valuable. This painting was purchased by my father some years ago as an investment rather than for display or enjoyment, and was kept locked in a vault.

We forgot to add this to the list of assets submitted to you. Does this affect my father's estate?

Thanks

Vincent

Attachment 2

Administration of Estates Act 1925

47 Statutory trusts in favour of issue and other classes of relatives of intestate.

(1) Where under this Part of this Act the residuary estate of an intestate, or any part thereof, is directed to be held on the statutory trusts for the issue of the intestate, the same shall be held upon the following trusts, namely:—

(i) In trust, in equal shares if more than one, for all or any the children or child of the intestate, living at the death of the intestate, who attain the age of **[F1** eighteen years**]** . . . , and for all or any of the issue living at the death of the intestate who attain the age of **[F1** eighteen years**]** . . . under that age of any child of the intestate who predeceases the intestate, such issue to take through all degrees, according to their stocks, in equal shares if more than one, the share which their parent would have taken if living at the death of the intestate, and so that **[F4** (subject to section 46A)**]** no issue shall take whose parent is living at the death of the intestate and so capable of taking;

(ii) The statutory power of advancement, and the statutory provisions which relate to maintenance and accumulation of surplus income, shall apply, but when an infant marries**[F5**, or forms a civil partnership,**]** such infant shall be entitled to give valid receipts for the income of the infant's share or interest; . . .

(iv) The personal representatives may permit any infant contingently interested to have the use and enjoyment of any personal chattels in such manner and subject to such conditions (if any) as the personal representatives may consider reasonable, and without being liable to account for any consequential loss.

(2) If the trusts in favour of the issue of the intestate fail by reason of no child or other issue attaining an absolutely vested interest—

(a) the residuary estate of the intestate and the income thereof and all statutory accumulations, if any, of the income thereof, or so much thereof as may not have been paid or applied under any power affecting the same, shall go, devolve and be held under the provisions of this Part of this Act as if the intestate had died without leaving issue living at the death of the intestate;

(b) references in this Part of this Act to the intestate 'leaving no issue' shall be construed as 'leaving no issue who attain an absolutely vested interest';

(c) references in this Part of this Act to the intestate 'leaving issue' or 'leaving a child or other issue' shall be construed as 'leaving issue who attain an absolutely vested interest.'

(3) Where under this Part of this Act the residuary estate of an intestate or any part thereof is directed to be held on the statutory trusts for any class of relatives of the intestate, other than issue of the intestate, the same shall be held on trusts corresponding to the statutory trusts for the issue of the intestate (other than the provision for bringing any money or property into account) as if such trusts (other than as aforesaid) were repeated with the substitution of references to the members or member of that class for references to the children or child of the intestate.

[F7 (4) References in paragraph (i) of subsection (1) of the last foregoing section to the intestate leaving, or not leaving, a member of the class consisting of brothers or sisters of the whole blood of the intestate and issue of brothers or sisters of the whole blood of the intestate shall be construed as references to the intestate leaving, or not leaving, a member of that class who attains an absolutely vested interest.**]**

[F8 (4A) Subsections (2) and (4) are subject to section 46A.**]**

[F9 (4B) Subsections (4C) and (4D) apply if a beneficiary under the statutory trusts—

(a) fails to attain an absolutely vested interest because the beneficiary dies without having reached 18 and without having married or formed a civil partnership, and

(b) dies leaving issue.

(4C) The beneficiary is to be treated for the purposes of this Part as having died immediately before the intestate.

(4D) The residuary estate (together with the income from it and any statutory accumulations of income from it) or so much of it as has not been paid or applied under a power affecting it is to devolve accordingly.**]**

* * *

■ YOUR TURN

Have a go at answering question 2, remembering the guidance on pages 1-3.

- Remember the structured approach in the SRA's assessment criteria on page 2.
- Consider the client's perspective at all times.
- Create a list of the most salient legal issues raised by the question, especially the assets and their value.
- Timings are important: you will need to prepare and write your answer in one hour.

SQE1 Functioning legal knowledge link

Remember from ***Revise SQE: Wills and Administration of Estates*** that any property held as joint tenants before death passes to a surviving joint tenant through survivorship, although there is still an impact on inheritance tax to consider (chapter 6). Revise the rules on intestacy in chapter 5, and how certain assets such as life assurance policies in trust pass outside an estate.

EVALUATING YOUR ANSWER

When you have attempted question 2, mark it yourself against the SQE2 case and matter analysis assessment criteria. Do you think your attempt met the threshold standard?

Now compare your attempt with the following key legal points and two sample answers to question 2. A circled number indicates that commentary is provided for this part of the answer. The commentary explains whether or not the sample satisfies the assessment criteria, and accordingly whether it is likely to meet the SQE2 threshold standard.

➡Key legal points: question 2

- Remember that the rules of intestacy apply when there is no will or a will is invalid. The former is relevant here as Vito died without a will.
- The rules on intestacy are statutory in nature and are found within the Administration of Estates Act 1925. The excerpt in Attachment 2 in relation to s 47 and statutory trusts is important given the large family remaining.
- If there is a surviving spouse or civil partner, they take a statutory legacy of £322,000 plus all personal chattels (belongings used in everyday life) and half of the residuary estate. As Carmela seems to have survived Vito (and must do so by 28 days) then distribution will follow as stated. Special notice needs to be taken of the Modigliani painting referred to in the email.
- The remainder of the estate is split between 'issue' – make sure you know how 'issue' is identified. If the 'issue' are minors, then the property may be held on statutory trust (under the Administration of Estates Act 1925), hence the excerpt in Attachment 2.
- You will need to take account of property falling outside the estate, such as life assurance policies in trust and co-owned property, and also explain the Modigliani investment (it is not a personal belonging).
- In intestacy cases, details of the family members are important to ascertain who receives assets. The question of intestacy is usually, like here, separate to the issue of inheritance tax.
- Keep in mind the specific questions asked by the partner and avoid going off on a tangent by providing information not pertinent to these questions.

■ SAMPLE ANSWER 1 TO QUESTION 2

You have asked me to advise Carmela Andolini regarding the estate of her late husband, Vito, who died intestate last month. It appears that Vito was a successful businessman who at the time of his death owned a number of assets including properties, cars and, according to the email from Vito and Carmela's son Vincent, an extremely valuable Modigliani painting that was purchased as an investment and kept in a vault. Vito also had a relatively large family, leaving a wife, his mother, children and grandchildren. ❶

Assets of Vito's succession estate

The first step is to remove all items which pass outside the estate, and then I will identify how those assets are distributed according to intestacy rules.

Items 1, 3, 6 and 11 fall outside the succession estate and can therefore be removed:

- Item 1: the apartment in Little Venice and its contents (£1,580,000)
- Item 3: the contents of the Wimbledon house (£100,000)
- Item 6: the NatWest savings account balance (£18,000). ❷

These three items were held as joint tenants, and as such the rules of survivorship apply as there is no evidence of severance before Vito's death. First, severance requires acting on one's own share, for example by mortgaging, leasing or selling. It is a unilateral act, but this has not occurred on the facts as we have them. Second, severance can be by either mutual conduct or mutual agreement where all joint tenants must either act or agree that the joint tenancy no longer exists; there is no evidence of this. Finally, severance can be in writing and, if it is, it must be served on remaining joint tenants demonstrating an immediate intention to sever; there is no evidence of this. As such, without such severance, the rules of survivorship state that all property jointly owned as joint tenants passes to the surviving joint tenant, automatically outside the estate and as such outside the rules of intestacy (Law of Property Act 1925). These three items will automatically vest in Carmela as the surviving joint tenant. All other items are said to be owned solely by Vito at the time of death. ❸

It should be noted, however, that joint tenant assets do not necessarily impact any inheritance tax calculations. Jointly held property may still attract inheritance tax but this is not a necessary part of the analysis here.

This totals **£1,698,000** thus far, covering items 1, 3 and 6.

Item 11 also falls outside the estate as it is a life assurance policy written in trust for Vito and Carmela's grandson, Frank. As Frank is a minor this will be held on trust until adulthood, in line with the policy details. At a later date we should advise the client that trustees will need to be appointed, but this is not pertinent to the client's immediate questions.

This totals another **£50,000** in relation to the policy.

Overall, **£1,748,000** is excluded from the estate in relation to intestacy rules. ❹

The succession estate contains the remaining items and is worth **£961,800**. This figure includes the unpaid salary owed to Vito at the date of his death, as sums owed to the deceased are treated as an asset. ❺

The cost of the funeral expenses (**£1,800**) is deducted to leave a net succession estate available for distribution of **£960,000**. ❻

Distribution of assets (including Modigliani painting)

I will deal with distribution of assets to Carmela first:

- As Vito's widow, and providing she has survived him by 28 days, Carmela will take a statutory legacy of the first **£322,000** of the value of the estate.
- She will also take all personal belongings – items 4, 8 and 9 – providing they were used by Vito in everyday life and not just investment items. These items total **£34,000**.
- The Modigliani painting does *not* qualify as a personal belonging because it was purchased as an investment, not displayed or enjoyed but rather kept in a vault. Personal belongings are defined as those that are used and enjoyed on a regular basis. As such, the painting will also fall into the death estate but is not included in the calculations here as it needs to be valued.
- Carmela will also receive half of the residue, which I have calculated as £302,000 as shown here:
  £960,000 – £322,000 – £34,000 = **£604,000 residue**
  Divided by 2 = **£302,000**
- In total Carmela will receive £322,000 + £34,000 + £302,000 = **£658,000.** (7)

The 'issue' will take the remaining half of the estate, £302,000:

- The issue would normally have been Sonny, Vincent and Connie on the statutory trusts. However, Sonny predeceased Vito, so his third of the residue (£100,666) passes to Frank contingent on reaching the age of 18. If Frank dies under 18 or without issue, his share would be divided between Vincent and Connie.
- Vincent would also take one-third (£100,666) as an adopted child is counted as 'issue'.
- Connie is aged 18, so she will also take one-third of the residue (£100,666). (8)

Vito has died with a surviving spouse and issue. This means that the 'intestacy flowchart' stops here and that Vito's mother and any other relative receive nothing. (9)

COMMENTARY

(1) The candidate gives a concise summary of the task they have been presented with. This is a good start, as this paragraph touches on all of the pertinent points that will contribute to the advice.

(2) The candidate begins their analysis strongly by explaining how assets may fall outside a deceased's estate. The items are clearly listed with values and explanations given as to why these joint tenancy assets fall outside the estate. This demonstrates the skill of using the materials effectively to draw accurate conclusions.

(3) The candidate recognises that intestacy rules are statutory; they highlight the relevant statute and case law in relation to joint tenancy, and successfully explain why these items fall outside the estate. The candidate clearly demonstrates their ability to apply relevant law to the facts of the scenario, as required by the assessment criteria.

(4) The candidate has been advised that they do not need to deal with inheritance tax. In this section they acknowledge this, whilst also demonstrating their knowledge that jointly held property may still attract inheritance tax. They also note that trustees will need to be appointed for item 11, but that this can be dealt with at a later date. This shows a mature and comprehensive grasp of the legal and procedural issues arising from this scenario, and in practice both of these points would be helpful for the next person dealing with this file.

(5) There is good detail here, with the candidate giving running totals and accurately calculating the assets that remain within the estate. This gives clarity to the client and demonstrates a client-focused approach.

6 There is good application to the scenario. Not only does the candidate effectively explain the assets falling within the estate but they also deduct the funeral expenses without speculating on other costs or debts, as the instructions clearly state. Again, the candidate provides clarity on the financial value, as the question demands.

7 The candidate has used the material effectively, calculating the figures correctly and explaining that Carmela takes a statutory legacy of £322,000, any personal belongings and half the residue. There is good application here of the principles and provisions of the Administration of Estates Act 1925. The painting is correctly identified as being an investment rather than a personal belonging, and the candidate explains why this is the case by applying the facts from the email to the legal status of the painting.

8 As above, the candidate shows excellent application of the Administration of Estates Act 1925 in relation to statutory trusts for issue, without falling into the trap of referring to 'marriage before 18'. This was originally included in the Act but has since been impliedly repealed by recent statute banning any marriage under 18 in England or Wales. The figures and the detail here are correct and impressively presented with great clarity - exactly as the question requires.

9 The candidate ends their advice clearly and succinctly, clarifying that Vito's mother and any other relative receive nothing under the intestacy rules. Plain and clear language is used, to make sure that the client will understand their position.

Does this answer meet the threshold?

The sample answer contains all of the information and application of the law on intestacy that the client requires and that the candidate has been asked to provide. The candidate discusses the relevant legislation and case law for rules of joint tenancy and survivorship, applying them to the scenario and reflecting upon those matters that are pertinent to the client's circumstances. The analysis is succinct and legally correct: the assets are analysed in detail and applied correctly, calculating the death estate with clear explanations. The answer is client-focused at all times and relevant to the facts of the scenario. It is therefore likely to meet the threshold standard for SQE2 case and matter analysis.

Now consider the second sample answer to question 2.

■ SAMPLE ANSWER 2 TO QUESTION 2

The estate

You have asked me to advise our new client, Carmel, about the estate of her late husband, Vito, who seemed to have died without making a will. This seems like a very difficult task, given the fact that Vito owned a large number of assets including cars, properties and a valuable Modigliani painting. He also had a large number of family members. The key questions seem to be the assets, the value of his estate and who will get what.

Items 1, 3, 6 and 11 fall outside the succession estate. These can be ignored for the purposes of his estate at the time of death.

The cottage plus contents, the savings account and contents of the house are owned as joint tenants with Carmela and therefore pass to her by survivorship. Carmeal will inherit the half share she does not already own for each of these assets. 1

The life assurance policy was written in trust for Frank, so he will receive £50,000 outside the succession estate. As he is a minor, the money will be held until he is old enough. 2

The succession estate contains the remaining items and is worth £961,800. This figure includes the unpaid salary owed at the date of his death, as sums owed to the deceased are treated as an asset. ❸

The cost of the funeral expenses, £1,800, is deducted to leave a net succession estate available for distribution of **£960,000**. There may be other debts that will have to be dealt with and deducted but it is unclear what they are on the facts. ❹

Distribution

Carmela inherits items passing outside the succession estate as set out above – worth £56,500 in total (£45,000 + £500 + £2,000 + £9,000). Frank receives the life assurance policy proceeds of £50,000.

Vito has died intestate, leaving a spouse and issue, so they share his succession estate. Vito's mother receives nothing.

Carmela as spouse receives:

- Personal chattels (items 4, 8 and 9, assuming no items were used for business purposes): £34,000.
- The Modigliani painting is not on the list of assets provided and it can therefore be assumed that this personal belonging will pass to Carmeal through intestacy rules. It therefore does not need to be added to the overall value of the estate.
- Statutory legacy £270,000.
- **One half** of the residue (£960,000 – £34,000 – £270,000). ❺

Sonny, Vincent and Connie are entitled to share in the **other half** of the residue on the statutory trusts as set out below:

1. Sonny predeceased Vito so his third share of half of the residue passes to Frank, contingent on him reaching the age of 18 or earlier marriage. If he dies under 18, without issue and unmarried, then his share is divided equally between Vincent and Connie. ❻
2. Vincent takes a vested interest in a third share of half of the residue.
3. Connie takes a vested interest in a third share of half of the residue due to the fact that she is 18 and married. ❼

COMMENTARY

❶ The candidate begins weakly by giving a very vague introduction that fails to use appropriate language (they refer to the deceased's and client's first names only) and does not set down exactly which assets may fall outside the deceased's estate. Although the candidate has selected the correct items, no values are mentioned, and there is insufficient detail in the explanation as to why these joint tenancy assets fall outside the estate. Survivorship is not explained, and the final sentence in relation to Carmela lacks clarity. Note that the candidate misspells Carmela's name several times in this response. Whilst this is not a fatal error, it shows a lack of attention to detail and accuracy, and gives a poor impression to the assessor.

❷ The candidate quickly moves on to the life assurance policy; there is little sign of structure in this answer and the candidate seems to include points at random. Although they recognise that intestacy rules are statutory, the candidate fails to highlight the relevant statute and case law in relation to a life assurance policy held in trust and does not demonstrate why these items fall outside the estate. The response requires much more detail and legal application here, and overall this answer is too brief.

3 Once again there is a lack of detail in the calculations: the candidate does not provide a running total or show how they have worked out which assets remain within the estate, and more information is required on the asset of the unpaid salary. This is not good practice and shows little consideration of the client's request for understanding the value of the estate.

4 There is a lack of application to the scenario. The figures are correct, but the candidate not only fails to give specific detail but also begins to discuss other debts when specifically instructed not to do so by the question. Remember to keep referring to the question to make sure that your response only addresses what is asked of you.

5 In addition to a very poor layout, the candidate here makes a major mistake in stating the statutory legacy of £270,000: this is old law and out of date, the figure now being £322,000. This is a grave error as the answer will be incorrectly calculated and the client misinformed. The candidate needed to explain clearly that Carmela takes a statutory legacy of £322,000, any personal belongings and half the residue, calculating each amount accurately and clearly. The answer relating to the Modigliani painting is inaccurate as this was not a personal belonging but an investment; as such, it does not pass automatically to Carmela but rather passes to the death estate. The candidate is therefore failing to meet the assessment criteria requirements of applying the principles and provisions of the Administration of Estates Act 1925 correctly and comprehensively.

6 The candidate makes a poor application of the Administration of Estates Act 1925 in relation to statutory trusts for issue and falls into the trap of referring to 'marriage before 18'; this was in the original Act but has since been impliedly repealed by recent statute banning marriage under 18 in England or Wales. The figures and the details here are therefore incorrect so once again this response is unclear and tainted by error.

7 Finally, the candidate ends the advice with an error as to the relevance of Connie's marriage (see above) and also fails to explain that adopted children (Vincent) are counted as issue. The candidate could have completed their advice by emphasising that Vito's mother and any other relative receive nothing under the intestacy rules.

Does this answer meet the threshold?

When assessing the second report against the SQE2 case analysis assessment criteria, it is unlikely that it would meet the threshold standard. The candidate has misinterpreted the law and made errors, especially in relation to the statutory legacy and marriage of a minor. The answer was also a little brief, poorly structured and carelessly presented, and the candidate fails to show a full understanding of how the facts of the case will affect the outcome of any claim to the estate by Carmela or the issue.

■ KEY POINT CHECKLIST

This chapter has covered the following key knowledge points:

- The SQE2 assessment criteria for case and matter analysis and how to apply them in the context of wills and the administration of estates.
- A suggested structure for approaching an SQE2 case and matter analysis question.
- Examples of case and matter analysis that are likely and unlikely to meet the threshold standard, with full commentary on their strengths and weaknesses.

■ SUMMARY AND REFLECTION

When approaching the SQE2 case and matter analysis, take plenty of time to read the question carefully, think about the legal points the question is asking of you and draw up a short plan to follow so that your answer will be logically and clearly structured.

The assessor will be judging your ability to apply the law both correctly and comprehensively. As well as pinpointing the relevant law, you will therefore need to explain how it can be applied to the wider context of the client's scenario and the more obvious specific points.

The best way to practise case and matter analysis is to identify the issues in a case and consider what law applies to those issues, then focus on the needs and situation of your client when forming your response.

Now take time to reflect and consider what you might still need to work on, and whether you feel completely confident in your case and matter analysis skills for this topic area.

2

Legal research

■ MAKE SURE YOU KNOW

This chapter covers the skill of legal research in the context of wills and the administration of estates ('wills'). Legal research in wills is one of the skills that may be assessed on day two of the SQE2 assessments (see the Introduction for more detail). Your functioning legal knowledge of wills is tested in this assessment, and you will have to demonstrate that you can apply relevant legal principles when conducting research. The assessment will require you to dissect and decipher material such as case law, statutes and academic journal articles in order to advise your client on what could be a niche area of wills. You are also thrown 'red herrings' in this assessment - material that simply is not relevant at all. You will need to work quickly to remove these irrelevant materials from your application.

Before attempting the questions in this chapter, familiarise yourself with the contents of ***Revise SQE: Wills and the Administration of Estates***, ***Revise SQE: Land Law***, ***Revise SQE: Trusts Law***, ***Revise SQE: Property Practice*** and ***Revise SQE Business Law and Practice***.

■ SQE ASSESSMENT ADVICE

As you work through this chapter, remember to pay particular attention in your revision to:

- selecting relevant information about the legal issue from the primary and/or secondary sources provided
- evaluating the sources for the correct evidence to support your answer, remembering that not all of the material will be relevant
- understanding the client's problem from their perspective, especially in relation to the distribution of assets, clauses of wills or inheritance tax
- using understandable and simple language to convey facts and information effectively
- using correct legal terminology but also making sure that a lay client will understand your use of legal terms such as executors, administrators, intestacy or statutory trusts
- ensuring your legal analysis is sufficiently detailed in the context of the facts of the case
- recognising any ethical or professional conduct issues in the question and including advice in your answer on how these can be addressed.

See the Appendix for the SRA's performance indicators in legal research and how to demonstrate your competency in this skill.

■ INTRODUCTION TO LEGAL RESEARCH IN WILLS

The ability to carry out legal research in a core area such as wills is a vital skill in any Day One Solicitor's armoury. The SQE2 assessment in legal research will contain a scenario that could be taken from day-to-day legal practice. This could map directly onto the SQE1 syllabus, such as intestacy or inheritance tax, but you may be given an exercise testing your research skills on off-syllabus topics such as secret trusts hidden in a will.

For this assessment, you will read a memo or email from a partner that asks you to conduct legal research, provide the correct legal knowledge for them to be able to advise a client and include the legal authorities in your answer to support this advice. You will not need to illustrate your research path. Whilst the question will give you some direction about the areas you need to cover in your legal research, you will be required to apply your knowledge of those areas and your understanding of the resources provided to the scenario, and then communicate the relevant information to the partner clearly and concisely in writing. This chapter will provide examples of how you can do this and meet the assessment criteria for SQE2 legal research at the same time.

To succeed in your SQE2 legal research assessment, try to approach the question in a structured manner. The following method might be useful:

1. Once you have read through all the documentation, make a note of the specific question(s) being asked.
2. Write down the key facts from the instructions that you feel are relevant to answer the question. Try to identify the main issues so that you know what to look for in the materials provided.
3. Check the dates of the sources and then write down the key law that you think is relevant from the extracts provided, ideally using primary sources (case law and/or statute) over secondary sources (such as academic articles) wherever possible.
4. Check that the law identified in point 3 above relates back to and answers the question(s) you identified in point 1.
5. Identify key steps applied in the relevant sources and write your answer to the question, ensuring it relates back to and answers the question(s) you identified in point 1 above.
6. Review your answer, keeping in mind the question and the SQE2 legal research assessment criteria.

Assessment technique

In this assessment you will need to draw on multiple sources of information to address the legal issue/client's problem effectively. It is vital not just to 'find' the relevant law but also to analyse it so that the client is left in no doubt as to their possible options. Write your answer with the client's needs at the forefront of your mind, and cite case law, sections of statute and secondary sources where relevant.

SQE2 legal research assessment criteria

Try to remember these points as you construct your response, and refer back to them as you review our sample answers in this chapter:

Skills

1. Identify and use relevant sources and information.
2. Provide advice which is client-focused and addresses the client's problem.
3. Use clear, precise, concise and acceptable language.

Application of law

4. Apply the law correctly to the client's situation.
5. Apply the law comprehensively to the client's situation.
6. Identify any ethical and professional conduct issues and exercise judgement to resolve them honestly and with integrity.

For more detailed support and guidance on how to meet the SQE2 legal research assessment criteria, see ***Introduction to Written Legal Skills for SQE2***, chapter 2, Legal research.

In ***Revise SQE: Wills and the Administration of Estates,*** chapter 5, we considered the rules relating to intestacy, and in chapter 6 those concerning property passing outside the estate. Remember that the research element of SQE2 may test you on an area that falls outside the scope of the areas of SQE1 FLK. The first question in this chapter, although within the broad heading of the practice area of wills, is *outside* the scope of the SQE1 FLK. The sample questions in the chapter include six or seven sources for you to consider, but bear in mind that the SQE2 assessment might include up to eight sources.

■ QUESTION 1

Email to candidate

From: Partner
Sent: 13 May 202#
To: Candidate
Subject: Elizabeth Tremain

You may remember that Elizabeth Tremain (aged 55) came to us for advice on the administration of her late husband Derek's estate, which included a five-bedroom property jointly registered in both their names. Derek left no will, and we have already advised her in relation to the general rules and principles of intestacy.

Once the property has been transferred into her sole name, Elizabeth (as sole surviving legal owner) is keen for it to stay in the family. She wants to put the property into joint ownership with her sister Anna (aged 47), so that she and Anna would be both joint owners and beneficial joint tenants on the title. She has instructed me to go ahead with the transfer, so for the purposes of this exercise please assume that this has already been done.

Elizabeth and Anna are due to go on holiday together abroad in a few months. Elizabeth is very anxious to know the implications for the property if anything were to happen to Anna and herself whilst they are away. She is trying to recover from a phobia about flying and would feel more confident about taking the flight if she could be reassured about the ownership of the house in the (highly unlikely) event of a plane crash that caused both their deaths.

Please research the effect of the property now being in joint names between Elizabeth and Anna on the following:

1. **In the event that Elizabeth and Anna die at different times.**
2. **In the event that Elizabeth and Anna die simultaneously.**

You should include, for my reference, your legal reasoning and mention any key sources or authorities.

Many thanks

Partner

Note to candidates:
Given the time constraints of this assessment, we have not provided the full text of some primary sources. Where the full text of a primary source is not provided, candidates

may nevertheless cite the primary source on the basis it is referred to in one or more of the secondary sources provided and the full text can be checked at a later date.

Information displayed is as obtained on the date of search, for example purposes only. Information herein is not to be relied upon outside the purposes of this sample question.

Attachments

You have been provided with the following sources listed alphabetically in order of source name. The order of presentation is not intended as a guide to the order in which they should be consulted.

PLEASE NOTE THAT PART OR ALL OF SOME OF THESE SOURCES MAY NOT BE RELEVANT TO ANSWERING THE QUESTION

1. 'English Commorientes and Joint Tenancies – A Fresh Look at Section 184 of the Law of Property Act 1925' (2019) *Trust Law International* 33(3), Mark Pawlowski and James Brown
2. *Estate of John William Scarle, deceased (by his personal representative Ann Winter) v Estate of Marjorie Ann Scarle, deceased (by her personal representative Deborah Ann Cutler)* [2019] EWHC 2224 (Ch)
3. Law of Property Act 1925 c 20 ss 34, 36, 184, 188
4. *Sen v Headley* [1991] Ch 425
5. *Stack v Dowden* [2007] UKHL 17 HL
6. Trusts of Land and Appointment of Trustees Act 1996 c 47 ss 11–14

* * *

Source 1

'English Commorientes and Joint Tenancies – A Fresh Look at Section 184 of the Law of Property Act 1925' (2019) *Trust Law International* 33(3), Mark Pawlowski and James Brown

The word 'commorientes' refers to the situation where two (or more) persons die in circumstances where it is uncertain which of them died last. Where there is uncertainty as to who was the last survivor, the effect of current English law is to prescribe artificially the sequence among consecutive deaths. Section 184 of the Law of Property Act 1925 provides a presumed order of succession based on seniority when the deaths have arisen in circumstances which render it uncertain which of two (or more) people survived the other(s). The presumption applies in cases of both testate and intestate [. . .] deaths and in respect of property held on a joint tenancy [. . .] where there is an automatic right of survivorship between the co-owners so that the last survivor of two (or more) tenants will become the sole owner of the property. The sequence of deaths is, therefore, particularly significant in determining the question of devolution where property is held on a joint tenancy. [. . .]

The standard of proof

Although the modern English cases, [. . .] as we have seen, have been reluctant to accept any evidence falling short of certainty as rebutting the statutory presumption under s 184, it is not entirely beyond the realms of possibility to envisage a case where the deaths are so contemporaneous as to warrant an actual finding of simultaneity. The difficulty, however, lies in the application of the correct standard of proof.

Most recently, HH Judge Kramer, in *Scarle v Scarle*, [. . .] has ruled that the appropriate standard is the civil standard of proof (ie the balance of probabilities). In this case, the husband, 79, and the wife, 69, both died of hypothermia. The wife had had limited mobility and the husband had been her carer. The husband's daughter was the claimant and the wife's daughter was the defendant. The husband was found in the lounge and the wife in the toilet area of their home.

However, the wife's walking frame was found next to the husband's body. There was evidence that the husband had been alive on the floor for some time before death. Both were in the early stages of decomposition, which appeared to be more advanced in the wife. Expert evidence was adduced as to the temperature and environmental conditions in the house because of their effect on the rate of decomposition, although it was agreed that decomposition alone was not determinative of the time of death. [. . .] In view of the uncertainties regarding the order of death, the presumption in s 184 was held to apply so that the wife was presumed to have survived her husband. [. . .]

Conclusion

A repeal of s 184 of the 1925 Act in relation to property held on a joint tenancy in favour of an automatic severance of the joint tenancy would, it is submitted, have at least two major advantages over the current law in England. First, no automatic right of survivorship would operate as between the various deceased favouring the youngest estate to the exclusion of all others. Secondly, all the respective successors would benefit equally in the estate thereby avoiding the current imbalance under s 184.

Any new enactment in this area (in place of s 184) should, however, cover the eventuality of both uncertainty in the order of death and simultaneous death. Statutory severance would not be triggered unless *all* of the joint tenants die in the same calamity. In cases of uncertainty, the burden of proof should be stated to be the civil standard on a balance of probabilities in line with the most recent [. . .] case law. Given also that, under the current law, the statutory presumption under s 184 may be excluded by a contrary testamentary provision, this exception should be retained in any new provision allowing for severance not to take place if a contrary intention is shown in the will of the deceased. [. . .] Additionally, the presumption of severance should be expressly extended to apply to the situation where the deaths all occur within a short interval of time. [. . .] The benefits of minimising costly and acrimonious litigation amongst family members seeking to prove that one of the deceased survived the other is, it is submitted, a strong policy consideration which favours the solution of automatic severance enabling equal distribution of the joint property.

The potential unfairness of applying the statutory presumption under s 184 is not, however, limited to cases of joint tenancies. If both deceased had made wills in favour of each other prior to their deaths or died intestate, the effect of s 184 is that the younger is presumed to have survived the older and thus become solely entitled to inherit under his (or her) will or intestacy.

Conversely, any legacy under the will of the younger in favour of the older lapses and falls into the younger person's residuary estate. Say, for example, an older brother and his younger sister die intestate in a common disaster where the order of deaths is uncertain. Let us also suppose that they both die without parents or issue owning separate property. Here, s 184 continues to apply so that the sister would inherit under her brother's intestacy. The brother's estate, on the other hand, would not take anything under his sister's intestacy as he is presumed to have died first. There is much, therefore, to be said for repealing s 184 altogether and replacing it with a statutory provision, along the lines of the American Uniform Simultaneous Death Act, which provides for the equal division of the deceased's estates in *all* cases of testate and intestate deaths (as well in respect of property held on a joint tenancy) unless the will of the deceased contains language otherwise dealing with the circumstance of simultaneous death.

* * *

Source 2

Estate of John William Scarle, deceased (by his personal representative Ann Winter) v Estate of Marjorie Ann Scarle, deceased (by her personal representative Deborah Ann Cutler) [2019] EWHC 2224 (Ch)

HH Judge Kramer:

1. On the 11 October 2016 John William Scarle, aged 79, and Marjorie Ann Scarle, a married couple, were found dead at their bungalow, 300 Eastwood Road North, Leigh on Sea, Essex. Mrs Scarle was the younger of the two, aged 69 at the time.
2. This case concerns the question as to which of them died first. The question is relevant as they were joint tenants of 300 Eastwood Road and the holders of a joint bank account with Co-op bank in which was deposited £18,000 at the time of the death. The law governing the ownership of jointly owned assets is that the last in time to die is entitled to the whole of the property and the sums in the account. As they have both died, the house and money will pass to those entitled to their estate, under the will of Mrs Scarle if her husband died first, or to those entitled on Mr Scarle's intestacy if he survived his wife. Central to this question is the operation of section 184 of the Law of Property Act 1925, a provision which, where the order of death is uncertain, creates a presumption that death occurred in order of seniority.

The Broad Dispute

3. Anna Winter is the only child of Mr Scarle and represents his estate. She is represented by Mr Wahiwala of counsel. Her case is that the presumption in s. 184 is not engaged if she proves on balance of probabilities, who died first. In the face of such proof it can no longer be said that the sequence of death is uncertain. She relies upon evidence which, she says, points to Mrs Scarle having been the first to die.
4. The Defendant, Deborah Ann Cutler, is the daughter of Mrs Scarle and represents her estate. She is represented by Mr Weale, of counsel. Her case is that in order for the presumption not to apply, Ms Winter has to prove that Mrs Scarle died first to a higher standard of proof, somewhere between proof

on balance of probabilities, the standard applied in civil proceedings, and beyond a reasonable doubt, the standard applied in criminal proceedings. Mr Weale says that whilst he is not arguing that the criminal standard of proof applies for the purposes of the hearing before me, he wishes to reserve his position on that argument in the event that the case goes further. He adds that, in any event, the claimant has not proved the sequence of deaths, even to the civil standard, and thus it is to be presumed that Mr Scarle died first.

5. In view of the importance that has been attached to the dispute as to the standard of proof required to avoid the operation of the presumption, it is convenient to look at that issue first.

The Law

6. Section 184 of the Law of Property Act 1925 states as follows:

> **'184. Presumption of survivorship in regard to claims to property.**
> In all cases where, after the commencement of this Act, two or more persons have died in circumstances rendering it uncertain which of them survived the other or others, such deaths shall (subject to any order of the court), for all purposes affecting the title to property, be presumed to have occurred in order of seniority, and accordingly the younger shall be deemed to have survived the elder.' [. . .]

7. Prior to the enactment of s. 184 there was no presumption of law as to survivorship based on age. The onus of proof was on the person asserting the affirmative. The question as to who survived was treated as a 'pure question of fact' to be proved by a 'clear preponderance of evidence' to support an inference as to who died first; see Wing v Angrave [1860] VIII H.L.C., 183, (1860) 11 E.R. 397 at p. 403 per Lord Campbell LC. The standard of proof adopted was the civil standard. In the absence of the presumption, in a case such as the present, in which there were cross-claims as to who was the survivor, if neither side could prove who died first their estate was distributed as if they had died at the same time. This approach produced results which may appear surprising, if not harsh. [. . .]

9. Mr Weale argues that s. 184 of the 1925 Act introduced a new code for ascertaining the order of death in cases of uncertainty which demands a higher standard of proof than that generally used in civil proceedings. He says that the use of the word 'uncertain' itself indicates that a standard of proof higher than the civil standard is required to render certain that which appears uncertain. In support of his arguments he relies upon Hickman v Peacey [1945] A.C. 304, Re Bate [1947] 2 All ER 418, Re Kennedy [2000] 2 I.R. 571 and the contrast with other statutory presumptions which provide for their rebuttal in terms such as '*unless the contrary is otherwise proved*', a formulation used in both Section 36 of the Road Traffic Act 1934 and Section 32 of the Mortgage Interest Restriction Act 1923 [. . .]

Conclusion

63. The only evidence which could point unequivocally to the sequence of death is the relative differences in decomposition, but does it? I am left with two not improbable explanations for this effect. The first is that Mrs Scarle predeceased her husband, the second that the micro-environment of the toilet area was warmer than the lounge. I cannot discount the latter in the absence of evidence from which I could reliably reach such a conclusion. Accordingly, I cannot fairly draw the inference that it was the former.

64. I can, and do, find that Mr and Mrs Scarle died of hypothermia at some time between 5th and 9th October 2016. The claimant has not satisfied me to the civil standard as to the order of death; it remains uncertain. Accordingly, the presumption of death in s. 184 of the Law of Property Act 1925 applies and Mrs Scarle is presumed to have survived Mr Scarle.

* * *

Source 3

Law of Property Act 1925 c 20 ss 34, 36, 184, 188

34 Effect of future dispositions to tenants in common

(1) An undivided share in land shall not be capable of being created except as provided by the Settled Land Act, 1925, or as hereinafter mentioned.

(2) Where, after the commencement of this Act, land is expressed to be conveyed to any persons in undivided shares and those persons are of full age, the conveyance shall (notwithstanding anything to the contrary in this Act) operate as if the land had been expressed to be conveyed to the grantees, or, if there are more than four grantees, to the four first named in the conveyance, as joint tenants **[F1** In trust for the persons interested in the land**]**.

Provided that, where the conveyance is made by way of mortgage the land shall vest in the grantees or such four of them as aforesaid for a term of years absolute (as provided by this Act) as joint tenants subject to cesser on redemption in like manner as if the mortgage money had belonged to them on a joint account, but without prejudice to the beneficial interests in the mortgage money and interest.

(3) A devise bequest or testamentary appointment, coming into operation after the commencement of this Act, of land to two or more persons in undivided shares shall operate as a devise bequest or appointment of the land to **F2** . . . the personal representatives of the testator, and **F2** . . . (but without prejudice to the rights and powers of the personal representatives for purposes of administration) **[F3** in trust for the persons interested in the land**]**.

[F4 (3A) In subsections (2) and (3) of this section references to the persons interested in the land include persons interested as trustees or personal representatives (as well as persons beneficially interested).**]**

F5(4) . . . .

Textual amendments

F1 Words in s. 34(2) substituted (1.1.1997) by 1996 c. 47, s. 5(1), Sch. 2 para. 3(2)(6) (with ss. 24(2), 25(4)); S.I. 1996/2974, art. 2.

F2 Words in s. 34(3) repealed (1.1.1997) by 1996 c. 47, ss. 5(1), 25(2), Sch. 2 para. 3(3)(a)(6), Sch. 4 (with ss. 24(2), 25(4)); S.I. 1996/2974, art. 2.

F3 Words in s. 34(3) substituted (1.1.1997) by 1996 c. 47, s. 5(1), Sch. 2 para. 3(3)(b)(6) (with ss. 24(2), 25(4)); S.I. 1996/2974, art. 2.

F4 S. 34(3A) inserted (1.1.1997) by 1996 c. 47, s. 5(1), Sch. 2 para. 3(4)(6) (with ss. 24(2), 25(4)); S.I. 1996/2974, art. 2

F5 S. 34(4) repealed (1.1.1997) by 1996 c. 47, ss. 5(1), 25(2), Sch. 2 para. 3(5)(6), Sch. 4 (with ss. 24(2), 25(4)); S.I. 1996/2974, art. 2.

36 Joint tenancies

(1) Where a legal estate (not being settled land) is beneficially limited to or held in trust for any persons as joint tenants, the same shall be held **[F1** in trust**]**, in like manner as if the persons beneficially entitled were tenants in common, but not so as to sever their joint tenancy in equity.

(2) No severance of a joint tenancy of a legal estate, so as to create a tenancy in common in land, shall be permissible, whether by operation of law or otherwise, but this subsection does not affect the right of a joint tenant to release his interest to the other joint tenants, or the right to sever a joint tenancy in an equitable interest whether or not the legal estate is vested in the joint tenants:

Provided that, where a legal estate (not being settled land) is vested in joint tenants beneficially, and any tenant desires to sever the joint tenancy in equity, he shall give to the other joint tenants a notice in writing of such desire or do such other acts or things as would, in the case of personal estate, have been effectual to sever the tenancy in equity, and thereupon **[F2** the land shall be held in trust on terms**]** which would have been requisite for giving effect to the beneficial interests if there had been an actual severance.

[F3 Nothing in this Act affects the right of a survivor of joint tenants, who is solely and beneficially interested, to deal with his legal estate as if it were not held **[F2** in trust**]**.**]**

(3) Without prejudice to the right of a joint tenant to release his interest to the other joint tenants no severance of a mortgage term or trust estate, so as to create a tenancy in common, shall be permissible.

Textual amendments

F1 Words in s. 36(1) substituted (1.1.1997) by 1996 c. 47, s. 5(1), Sch. 2 para. 4(2)(4) (with ss. 24(2), 25(4)); S.I. 1996/2974, art. 2.

F2 Words in s. 36(2) substituted (1.1.1997) by 1996 c. 47, s. 5(1), Sch. 2 para. 4(3)(a)(b)(4) (with ss. 24(2), 25(4)); S.I. 1996/2974, art. 2.

F3 Words added by Law of Property (Amendment) Act 1926 (c. 11), Sch.

184 Presumption of survivorship in regard to claims to property

In all cases where, after the commencement of this Act, two or more persons have died in circumstances rendering it uncertain which of them survived the other or others, such deaths shall (subject to any order of the court), for all purposes affecting the title to property, be presumed to have occurred in order of seniority, and accordingly the younger shall be deemed to have survived the elder.

188 Power to direct division of chattels

[F1(1)**]** Where any chattels belong to persons in undivided shares, the persons interested in a moiety or upwards may apply to the court for an order for division of the chattels or any of them, according to a valuation or otherwise, and the court may make such order and give any consequential directions as it thinks fit.

[F2(2) The county court has jurisdiction under this section where the amount or value of the property or of the interest in the property which is to be dealt with in the court does not exceed **[F3** £30,000**].]**

Textual amendments

F1 S. 188 renumbered as subsection (1) of that section by County Courts Act 1984 (c. 28, SIF 34), s. 148(1), Sch. 2 Pt. II para. 8(1).

F2 S. 188(2) added by County Courts Act 1984 (c. 28, SIF 34), s. 148(1), Sch. 2 Pt. II para. 8(2).

F3 Words in s. 188(2) substituted (1.7.1991) by S.I. 1991/724, art. 2(8), Sch. Pt. I.

* * *

Source 4

Sen v Headley [1991] Ch 425

LORD JUSTICE NOURSE

Donationes mortis causa may be said to have been an anomaly in our law, both for their immunity to the Statute of Frauds 1677 and the Wills Act 1837 and as exceptions to the rule that there is no equity to perfect an imperfect gift. But both Lord Hardwicke and Lord Eldon, while making to regret the doctrine, established extensions of it beyond a simple gift of a chattel by its delivery; the former to a gift of money secured by a bond, by delivery of the bond; the latter to a gift of money secured by a mortgage of land, by delivery of the mortgage deed. Later decisions have included gifts of other choses in action by delivery of the essential indicia of title. What has never before been directly decided in England is whether the doctrine applies to a gift of land by delivery of the title deeds. Lord Eldon undoubtedly thought that it did not, a view which has generally been assumed to be correct. Now Mr. Justice Mummery has given a decision in line with that assumption and we have to say whether we agree with him or not.

The facts of the case are set out in the judgment of the learned judge [1990] Ch. 728 and need not be repeated at length. Their essentials, which can be stated mainly in the judge's own words, are these. At his death aged 80 on 7th December 1986 the late Mr. Vivian 'Bob' Hewett was the owner of an unregistered freehold house, 56 Gordon Road, Ealing, London W5, a substantial, detached, suburban property in a dilapidated condition. He had bought the house in 1936 for £1,100. Before the judge it was estimated to be worth several hundred thousand pounds, being the principal asset of an estate which was sworn for probate purposes at just under £315,000. Mr. Hewett had been married, but had

had no children. After many years of separation, he and his wife were divorced in 1977. For over 30 years Mr. Hewett had enjoyed a close friendship with the plaintiff, Mrs. Margaret Sen. For about ten years from the end of 1954 they lived together as man and wife. Although from about 1964 onwards Mrs. Sen saw less of Mr. Hewett, the judge accepted her evidence that their relationship continued to be a close one and that it could not have been closer if they had actually been husband and wife.

Early in November 1986 Mr. Hewett was admitted to the Hammersmith Hospital suffering from an inoperable cancer of the pancreas. He was informed that his condition would inexorably deteriorate. While he was there Mrs. Sen visited him every day. She also looked after his house, to which she had always had her own set of keys. Amongst the things which he asked her to bring to the hospital was a bunch of keys kept in a drawer of the sideboard. Mr. Hewett wanted to go home to die and on 26th November he left the Hammersmith Hospital. On 2nd December he collapsed on the floor of his bedroom and was admitted to the Ealing Hospital, where Mrs. Sen continued to visit him every day in a room of his own. Mr. Hewett knew that he did not have long to live.

On 4th December, three days before his death and when they were alone together, Mrs. Sen asked Mr. Hewett what she should do about the house if anything should happen to him. Mr. Hewett replied: 'The house is yours, Margaret. You have the keys. They are in your bag. The deeds are in the steel box'. When she asked about the contents of the house, he said: 'Do what you like. It's all yours.' Nothing more was said between them about the subject of the house or its contents.

After Mr. Hewett's death Mrs. Sen found in her handbag the bunch of keys which she had brought to the Hammersmith Hospital at his request. She did not know how they came to be there, but believed that Mr. Hewett must have slipped them into the handbag, without her noticing, on one of her many visits to the hospital. In any event, the judge, who accepted Mrs. Sen's evidence throughout, found that Mr. Hewett had delivered the bunch of keys to Mrs. Sen, being the keys referred to by him on 4th December. One of them was what appears to have been the only key to the locked steel box in which the title deeds to the house were kept. Another was the key to a cupboard in the house in which Mrs. Sen found the box a day or two after Mr. Hewett's death. She was not sure whether the cupboard was locked or unlocked. But when she unlocked the box the deeds were inside.

Mr. Hewett died intestate. His next of kin are a sister who lives in South Africa, a nephew who lives in Vancouver and a niece who lives in Brighton. The writ was issued on 13th October 1987. Letters of administration to the estate have since been freshly granted to the nephew, who is now the defendant in the action. Mrs. Sen claims that Mr. Hewett made her a donatio mortis causa of the house by constructive delivery of the title deeds, the only key of the steel box in which they were kept having been delivered to her before Mr. Hewett uttered the words of gift on 4th December. Mr. Hewett having at all times retained his own set of keys to the house, no claim has been made in respect of the contents. For reasons which will appear incidentally in due course, it could not have been argued that there was any delivery of the contents.

There have been several judicial statements of what, in general terms, is necessary to constitute a donatio mortis causa: *Cain v. Moon* (1896), 2 QB 283, 285 (Lord Russell of Killowen C.J.); *re Craven's Estate* (1937) Ch. 423, 426 (Farwell J.); and *Delgoffe v. Fader* (1939) Ch. 922, 927 (Luxmoore L.J.). Regard must also be had to what was said by this court in *Birch v. Treasury Solicitor* (1951) Ch. 298, the most authoritative of the modern decisions. If the question whether the subject matter is capable of passing by way of donatio mortis causa is put on one side, the three general requirements for such a gift may be stated very much as they are stated in *Snell's Equity*, 29th ed., 380-383. First, the gift must be made in contemplation, although not necessarily in expectation, of impending death. Secondly, the gift must be made upon the condition that it is to be absolute and perfected only on the donor's death, being revocable until that event occurs and ineffective if it does not. Thirdly, there must be a delivery of the subject matter of the gift, or the essential indicia of title thereto, which amounts to a parting with dominion and not mere physical possession over the subject matter of the gift.

The trial extended over three days in November 1989, with judgment being reserved. Mr. Justice Mummery gave a very careful judgment. He found no difficulty in holding that the first and second requirements were satisfied on the evidence and that part of his decision has not been questioned. At page 736 B-C he said:

> 'The real difficulty in this case is caused by the third requirement which raises acutely the question whether it can ever be complied with in the case of real property when all that has occurred is an informal delivery of title deeds, or the means of access to the title deeds, accompanied by oral words of gift.'

It was largely because the judge, after a conscientious review of English and Commonwealth authorities and texts, was of the opinion that that difficulty had not been overcome that he dismissed the action. He also regarded it as an area where judicial caution and certainty of precedent were appropriate and as one where the policy of the law in regard to the formalities for the creation and transmission of interests in land should be upheld. Against the judge's decision Mrs. Sen has now appealed to this court.

* * *

Source 5

Stack v Dowden [2007] UKHL 17 HL

LORD HOFFMANN

My Lords,

1. I have had the advantage of reading in draft the opinion of my noble and learned friend Baroness Hale of Richmond, and for the reasons she gives I too would dismiss the appeal. [...]

BARONESS HALE OF RICHMOND

My Lords,

40. The issue before us is the effect of a conveyance into the joint names of a cohabiting couple, but without an explicit declaration of their respective beneficial interests, of a dwelling house which was to become their home. This is, so far as I am aware, the first time that this issue has come before the House, whether the couple be married or, as in this case, unmarried. The principles of law are the same, whether or not the couple are married, although the inferences to be drawn from their conduct may be different: *Bernard v Josephs* [1982] Ch 391, *per* Griffiths LJ at 402. [...]

60. [. . .] There is no need for me to rehearse all the developments in the case law since *Pettitt v Pettitt* and *Gissing v Gissing*, discussed over more than 70 pages following the quoted passage, by Chadwick LJ in *Oxley v Hiscock* [2004] EWCA Civ 546, [2005] Fam 211, and most importantly by my noble and learned friend, Lord Walker of Gestingthorpe in his opinion, which make good that proposition. The law has indeed moved on in response to changing social and economic conditions. The search is to ascertain the parties' shared intentions, actual, inferred or imputed, with respect to the property in the light of their whole course of conduct in relation to it. [. . .]
62. Furthermore, although the parties' intentions may change over the course of time, producing what my noble and learned friend, Lord Hoffmann, referred to in the course of argument as an 'ambulatory' constructive trust, at any one time their interests must be the same for all purposes. They cannot at one and the same time intend, for example, a joint tenancy with survivorship should one of them die while they are still together, a tenancy in common in equal shares should they separate on amicable terms after the children have grown up, and a tenancy in common in unequal shares should they separate on acrimonious terms while the children are still with them. [. . .]
64. The majority of cases reported since *Pettitt* and *Gissing* have concerned homes conveyed into the name of one party only and it is in that context that the more flexible approach to quantification identified by Chadwick LJ in *Oxley v Hiscock* has emerged: see, in particular, *Grant v Edwards* [1986] Ch 638, described by Chadwick LJ as 'an important turning point' and referred to with 'obvious approval' in *Lloyds Bank plc v Rosset* [1991] 1 AC 107, *Stokes v Anderson* [1991] 1 FLR 391, *Midland Bank plc v Cooke* [1995] 4 All ER 562, and *Drake v Whipp* [1996] 1 FLR 826.
65. Curiously, it is in the context of homes conveyed into joint names but without an express declaration of trust that the courts have sometimes reverted to the strict application of the principles of the resulting trust: see *Walker v Hall* [1984] FLR 126 and two cases decided by the same court on the same day, *Springette v Defoe* [1992] 2 FLR 388 and *Huntingford v Hobbs* [1993] 1 FLR 736; but cf *Crossley v Crossley* [2005] EWCA Civ 1581, [2006] 2 FLR 813. However, Chadwick LJ commented in *Oxley v Hiscock* [2005] Fam 211, at 235:

> 47. It is, I think, important to an understanding of the reasoning in the judgments in *Springette v Defoe* that each member of this court seems to have thought that when Lord Bridge referred, in *Lloyds Bank plc v Rosset* [1991] 1 AC 107, 132F, to the need to base a 'finding of an agreement or arrangement to share in this sense' on 'evidence of express discussions between the partners' he was addressing the secondary, or consequential, question – 'what was the common intention of the parties as to the extent of their respective beneficial interests' – rather than the primary, or threshold, question – 'was there a common intention that each should have a beneficial interest in the property?' [. . .]

69. In law, 'context is everything' and the domestic context is very different from the commercial world. Each case will turn on its own facts. Many more factors than financial contributions may be relevant to divining the parties' true intentions. These include: any advice or discussions at the time of the transfer which cast light upon their intentions then; the reasons why the home was acquired in their joint names; the reasons why (if it be the case) the survivor was authorised to give a receipt for the capital moneys; the purpose for which the home was acquired; the nature of the parties' relationship; whether they had children for whom they both had responsibility to provide a home; how the purchase was financed, both initially and subsequently; how the parties

arranged their finances, whether separately or together or a bit of both; how they discharged the outgoings on the property and their other household expenses. When a couple are joint owners of the home and jointly liable for the mortgage, the inferences to be drawn from who pays for what may be very different from the inferences to be drawn when only one is owner of the home. The arithmetical calculation of how much was paid by each is also likely to be less important. It will be easier to draw the inference that they intended that each should contribute as much to the household as they reasonably could and that they would share the eventual benefit or burden equally. The parties' individual characters and personalities may also be a factor in deciding where their true intentions lay. In the cohabitation context, mercenary considerations may be more to the fore than they would be in marriage, but it should not be assumed that they always take pride of place over natural love and affection. At the end of the day, having taken all this into account, cases in which the joint legal owners are to be taken to have intended that their beneficial interests should be different from their legal interests will be very unusual.

70. This is not, of course, an exhaustive list. There may also be reason to conclude that, whatever the parties' intentions at the outset, these have now changed. An example might be where one party has financed (or constructed himself) an extension or substantial improvement to the property, so that what they have now is significantly different from what they had then.

* * *

Source 6

Trusts of Land and Appointment of Trustees Act 1996 c 47 ss 11–14

11 Consultation with beneficiaries

(1) The trustees of land shall in the exercise of any function relating to land subject to the trust—
  - (a) so far as practicable, consult the beneficiaries of full age and beneficially entitled to an interest in possession in the land, and
  - (b) so far as consistent with the general interest of the trust, give effect to the wishes of those beneficiaries, or (in case of dispute) of the majority (according to the value of their combined interests).

(2) Subsection (1) does not apply—
  - (a) in relation to a trust created by a disposition in so far as provision that it does not apply is made by the disposition,
  - (b) in relation to a trust created or arising under a will made before the commencement of this Act, or
  - (c) in relation to the exercise of the power mentioned in section 6(2).

(3) Subsection (1) does not apply to a trust created before the commencement of this Act by a disposition, or a trust created after that commencement by reference to such a trust, unless provision to the effect that it is to apply is made by a deed executed—
  - (a) in a case in which the trust was created by one person and he is of full capacity, by that person, or

(b) in a case in which the trust was created by more than one person, by such of the persons who created the trust as are alive and of full capacity.

(4) A deed executed for the purposes of subsection (3) is irrevocable.

12 The right to occupy

(1) A beneficiary who is beneficially entitled to an interest in possession in land subject to a trust of land is entitled by reason of his interest to occupy the land at any time if at that time—
(a) the purposes of the trust include making the land available for his occupation (or for the occupation of beneficiaries of a class of which he is a member or of beneficiaries in general), or
(b) the land is held by the trustees so as to be so available.

(2) Subsection (1) does not confer on a beneficiary a right to occupy land if it is either unavailable or unsuitable for occupation by him.

(3) This section is subject to section 13.

13 Exclusion and restriction of right to occupy

(1) Where two or more beneficiaries are (or apart from this subsection would be) entitled under section 12 to occupy land, the trustees of land may exclude or restrict the entitlement of any one or more (but not all) of them.

(2) Trustees may not under subsection (1)—
(a) unreasonably exclude any beneficiary's entitlement to occupy land, or
(b) restrict any such entitlement to an unreasonable extent.

(3) The trustees of land may from time to time impose reasonable conditions on any beneficiary in relation to his occupation of land by reason of his entitlement under section 12.

(4) The matters to which trustees are to have regard in exercising the powers conferred by this section include—
(a) the intentions of the person or persons (if any) who created the trust,
(b) the purposes for which the land is held, and
(c) the circumstances and wishes of each of the beneficiaries who is (or apart from any previous exercise by the trustees of those powers would be) entitled to occupy the land under section 12.

(5) The conditions which may be imposed on a beneficiary under subsection (3) include, in particular, conditions requiring him—
(a) to pay any outgoings or expenses in respect of the land, or
(b) to assume any other obligation in relation to the land or to any activity which is or is proposed to be conducted there.

(6) Where the entitlement of any beneficiary to occupy land under section 12 has been excluded or restricted, the conditions which may be imposed on any other beneficiary under subsection (3) include, in particular, conditions requiring him to—
(a) make payments by way of compensation to the beneficiary whose entitlement has been excluded or restricted, or
(b) forgo any payment or other benefit to which he would otherwise be entitled under the trust so as to benefit that beneficiary.

(7) The powers conferred on trustees by this section may not be exercised—
(a) so as prevent any person who is in occupation of land (whether or not by reason of an entitlement under section 12) from continuing to occupy the land, or
(b) in a manner likely to result in any such person ceasing to occupy the land,
unless he consents or the court has given approval.

(8) The matters to which the court is to have regard in determining whether to give approval under subsection (7) include the matters mentioned in subsection (4) (a) to (c).

14 Applications for order

(1) Any person who is a trustee of land or has an interest in property subject to a trust of land may make an application to the court for an order under this section.

(2) On an application for an order under this section the court may make any such order—

(a) relating to the exercise by the trustees of any of their functions (including an order relieving them of any obligation to obtain the consent of, or to consult, any person in connection with the exercise of any of their functions), or

(b) declaring the nature or extent of a person's interest in property subject to the trust, as the court thinks fit.

(3) The court may not under this section make any order as to the appointment or removal of trustees.

(4) The powers conferred on the court by this section are exercisable on an application whether it is made before or after the commencement of this Act.

* * *

YOUR TURN

Have a go at answering question 1, remembering the guidance on pages 24–26.

- Remember the structured approach in the SRA's assessment criteria on page 25.
- Create a list of the relevant answers to the legal points raised in your instructions and addressed in the sources, remembering to use primary sources over secondary sources wherever possible.
- Evaluate the sources, and remember that some of them may not be relevant to your answer.
- Timings are important: you will need to prepare and write your answer in one hour.

SQE1 Functioning legal knowledge link

Remember from ***Revise SQE: Wills and Administration of Estates***, chapter 5, that the rules of intestacy apply when the deceased leaves no will; and, from chapter 6, that property held as joint tenants before death passes to a surviving joint tenant through survivorship.

EVALUATING YOUR ANSWER

When you have attempted question 1, mark it yourself against the SQE2 legal research assessment criteria. Do you think your attempt met the threshold standard?

Now compare your attempt with the following key legal points and two sample answers to question 1. A circled number indicates that commentary is provided for this part of the answer. The commentary explains whether or not the sample satisfies the assessment criteria, and accordingly whether it is likely to meet the SQE2 threshold standard.

➥Key legal points: question 1

In this assessment, part, or all, of the following sources are relevant to the question:

- 'English Commorientes and Joint Tenancies - A Fresh Look at Section 184 of the Law of Property Act 1925' (2019) *Trust Law International* 33(3), Mark Pawlowski and James Brown
- *Estate of John William Scarle, deceased (by his personal representative Ann Winter) v Estate of Marjorie Ann Scarle, deceased (by her personal representative Deborah Ann Cutler)* [2019] EWHC 2224 (Ch)
- Law of Property Act 1925 c 20 ss 36, 184
- *Stack v Dowden* [2007] UKHL 17 HL

The following sources are not relevant to the question:

- *Sen v Headley* [1991] Ch 425
- Trusts of Land and Appointment of Trustees Act 1996 c 47 ss 11–14

Key legal points include the following:

- Ordinarily, if Derek died without a will, intestacy rules would apply and Elizabeth would take the property as the surviving spouse. She was nevertheless a legal joint tenant with Derek before his death.
- Elizabeth would also take the property automatically under the rules of survivorship outside the intestacy rules. She would then become the sole legal owner and be free to deal with the property as she sees fit.
- When Anna has been added as a second legal owner, the focus of the question is the effect on the property of Elizabeth and Anna dying together at exactly the same time or at different times. This is where the research takes effect as this is largely outside the FLK required for SQE1.
- The answer is based on the rule of *commorientes* under s 184 of the Law of Property Act 1925: if joint tenants die together, the property is automatically vested in the estate of the youngest of the joint tenants. The cases of *Scarle* and *Stack v Dowden* are relevant here, as is the Law of Property Act 1925. However, the case of *Sen v Headley* and the Trusts of Land and Appointment of Trustees Act 1996 are not relevant to this question.
- Remember that the question only requires you to research this problem, but you should apply your FLK1 knowledge to fully understand the context of the question.

■ SAMPLE ANSWER 1 TO QUESTION 1

Our client, Elizabeth, is recently widowed. She jointly owned a property with her husband. We have advised her on the advantages of becoming joint tenant with her sister, Anna, and owning the property together. Elizabeth is seeking further advice on the future ownership of her property, in the event of the two sisters dying at the same time under the same circumstances, and how this affects the rule of survivorship. The law relating to the doctrine of survivorship should be applied to this situation. Under the survivorship rules, where one joint tenant dies, the surviving joint tenant will take the property absolutely. ❶

Where two or more people own a property together there is a separation of their legal and equitable ownership under section 34 of the Law of Property Act 1925 (LPA). If Elizabeth and Anna become joint legal owners of the property, they can only hold legal title as joint tenants (s 34 LPA 1925) ❷ but their equitable ownership can be held as joint tenants in undivided shares (*Stack v Dowden* [2007] UKHL 17 HL) or as tenants in common. If property is held as joint tenants, 'shares' of that property cannot be left in a will as both joint tenants are said to jointly own 100% of the property with no division of interests. ❸

Survivorship

Usually, the rules on survivorship mean that the last surviving joint tenant will somewhat arbitrarily take the property as the sole surviving joint tenant (s 36 LPA). Mark Pawlowski and James Brown confirm in their article 'English Commorientes and Joint Tenancies - A Fresh Look at Section 184 of the Law of Property Act 1925' that 'a presumed order of succession based on seniority' takes place. This rule will always favour the youngest joint tenant as they would in normal circumstances be the last to die. (4)

Under normal circumstances, therefore, if Elizabeth and Anna take the property as beneficial joint tenants then, in the ordinary course of events, Elizabeth (aged 55) would be outlived by Anna (aged 47). As such the property under the rules of survivorship would vest entirely in Anna, just as the property has vested in Elizabeth after the death of her joint tenant husband. (5)

Simultaneous death of the beneficial joint tenants

The client is concerned about what happens if she and her sister were to die instantly and together. This obscure part of English property law dealing with simultaneous deaths is found under s 184 LPA, named by Pawlowski and Brown as the *'commorientes'* rule:

> In all cases where, after the commencement of this Act, two or more persons have died in circumstances rendering it uncertain which of them survived the other or others, such deaths shall (subject to any order of the court), for all purposes affecting the title to property, be presumed to have occurred in order of seniority, and accordingly the younger shall be deemed to have survived the elder.

This means that, if both joint tenants die instantly and at the same time, the property goes in full to the estate of the youngest tenant, as they are presumed to be the last to die in the ordinary course of events. In this case, the property would vest entirely in Anna and her estate. (6)

Presumption rebutted?

There is a legal question as to whether the presumption can be rebutted by evidence, such as hypothetically whether Anna would have been the one to die first, for example due to an ongoing fatal illness. The most recent and fascinating case on this point is *Scarle v Scarle* [2019] EWHC 2224 (Ch), where a married couple both died and were discovered in the family home. Forensics could not decipher who had died first, as both bodies were so decomposed. The argument arose as the couple had children from earlier marriages and Mr Scarle died intestate, whereas Mrs Scarle had left a will. The order of death was needed in relation to the distribution of assets. The court decided that the burden of proof is civil - on the balance of probabilities - and it was as such impossible to establish on these facts. The *commorientes* rule applied and the property passed to Mrs Scarle's daughter as the youngest of the couple. (7)

Conclusion

It would seem that, under normal circumstances, without any rebuttable evidence to the contrary, if Elizabeth and Anna were beneficial joint tenants then, in the ordinary course of events, Elizabeth, as the older sister (aged 55) would be outlived by Anna (aged 47) and the property would vest in Anna. As such if the sisters as joint tenants were to die at the same time, the *commorientes* rule would apply and Anna as the younger sister would have the property vested in her estate. This would only be rebutted by evidence that, for example, due to some diagnosed pre-existing illness, Anna would have predeceased her older sister. On the facts this does not seem to be the case. (8)

COMMENTARY

1. Survivorship is clearly the issue here, and the candidate needs to recognise that there are two possible examples of survivorship - first between Derek and Elizabeth and then in relation to Elizabeth and Anna. The candidate has correctly not taken up too much time discussing the former, demonstrating that they can focus only on relevant material; there is no need to discuss the property moving from Derek. The real issue is how this doctrine operates if Elizabeth and Anna, as potential joint tenants at the point of death, die simultaneously. This is a good opening paragraph that pinpoints the main issue and sets up the rest of the answer.
2. Again, the candidate has pointed to the correct law under the Law of Property Act 1925, but only in so much as to set the context. This is excellent application of relevant legal sources.
3. The candidate has once again used the source material effectively with brief reference to *Stack v Dowden*, to explain the context that Elizabeth and Anna would be joint tenants and survivorship would normally apply. This demonstrates client-focused advice.
4. It is good practice to use secondary sources if it assists with explanation of a point of law or procedure. The candidate recognises that the article by Pawlowski and Brown was useful and relevant, and cites the article and the authors effectively. It is always recommended to use primary sources rather than secondary, but this is appropriate here.
5. The candidate has used the material effectively: they have spotted the ages of the two sisters and applied them to the case facts, to ensure that the correct and accurate advice is given to the client. Although not relevant to this particular question, this presents Elizabeth with an informed choice of whether Anna is the 'right' joint tenant to choose because she is the youngest sister (and therefore would inherit).
6. The '*commorientes*' rule is the key to answering this question, and the candidate has done well to find the rule in the source materials and cite the relevant section: s 184 LPA 1925. This provision is explained with clarity and applied to the facts of the case.
7. It is always good practice and effective advice to find and explain any exceptions to rules of law and procedure, and the rebuttal of the presumption of *commorientes* is an important factor here. The candidate again manages this effectively and refers to the key case of *Scarle v Scarle* to explain the possible rebuttal here, but without delving too deeply as there is no suggestion of a possibility of rebuttal on the facts.
8. Finally, the candidate demonstrates good practice in drawing an appropriate conclusion to ensure that the actual question is answered.

Does this answer meet the threshold?

The sample answer contains all of the information that the client requires and that the candidate has been asked to provide. It discusses the relevant legislation under the Law of Property Act 1925, especially s 184, and key case law such as *Scarle* and academic commentary by Pawlowski and Brown. The candidate selects the relevant sources for this question, shows how they apply to the scenario and does not mention the two irrelevant sources supplied in the materials. This response is clear, succinct and legally correct, and is therefore likely to meet the threshold standard for SQE2 legal research.

Now consider the second sample answer to question 1.

■ SAMPLE ANSWER 2 TO QUESTION 1

This case is based on the doctrine of survivorship, and the key issue is that of joint tenancy and how owners can protect their proprietary rights. ❶

Derek and Elizabeth were joint owners before Derek died, and so when he died his share would have passed to Elizabeth through the rules of intestacy: where there is no will, the surviving spouse takes the estate in full if there is no issue. Elizabeth would be able to deal with the property as she pleases under the Trusts of Land and Appointment of Trustees Act 1996. ❷ However, the client wishes to know whether she can add Anna to the title: as legal owner she can do so, and then they would also be legal joint tenants in undivided shares (*Stack v Dowden* [2007] UKHL 17 HL). Elizabeth, however, could not then leave shares in a will as Elizabeth and Anna would hold the property together. They would also be joint tenants of their equitable interests automatically and the rule of survivorship would apply. Section 14 of Trusts of Land and Appointment of Trustees Act 1996 states: '(1) Any person who is a trustee of land or has an interest in property subject to a trust of land may make an application to the court for an order under this section.' The case of *Sen v Headley* [1991] Ch 425 also deals with gifts given in contemplation of death. ❸

Survivorship

It would seem then that, if Elizabeth and Anna are joint tenants, the last surviving joint tenant would take the property, as explained by Mark Pawlowski. If Elizabeth survives Anna, then Elizabeth's estate will take the property. However, if they both die together, then, Pawlowski explains, the estate will vest in the youngest joint tenant as they are expected to die first in normal circumstances. ❹ This will be explained further below.

In relation to Elizabeth and Anna, if they take the property as beneficial joint tenants then in the ordinary course of events, Elizabeth (47) would outlive Anna (55) and as such the property under the rules of survivorship would vest entirely in Elizabeth, just as the property had already vested in Elizabeth after the death of her husband. ❺

Simultaneous death of the beneficial joint tenants

The question, though, is what happens if the sisters die together and at the same time. This is known as the '*commorientes*' rule dealing with simultaneous deaths. It can be found under s 184 LPA: 'In all cases where, after the commencement of this Act, two or more persons have died in circumstances rendering it uncertain which of them survived the other or others, such deaths shall (subject to any order of the court), for all purposes affecting the title to property, be presumed to have occurred in order of seniority, and accordingly the younger shall be deemed to have survived the elder.' This means that the property would vest entirely in Elizabeth and her estate. ❻

Conclusion

It would seem that, if the two sisters died together at the same time, then Elizabeth as the younger sister would take the property under the *commorientes* rule. It should be noted, though, that this would not really change the situation as Elizabeth at the time of her husband's death is already the sole surviving joint tenant. The order here would be important, as in *Scarle v Scarle* [2019] EWHC 2224 (Ch). ❼

COMMENTARY

1. This statement is not correct, as the candidate has confused the focus of the question. Survivorship is clearly the key issue here, but the candidate has placed the emphasis on joint tenancy and protection of rights. This indicates that the advice to follow might not be client-focused, as required by the assessment criteria.
2. The candidate has made two errors here: (1) because Elizabeth and Derek were joint tenants, intestacy is not strictly relevant so the property would pass to Elizabeth *outside* the rules of intestacy; (2) for the same reason, Elizabeth would not need to rely on the Trusts of Land and Appointment of Trustees Act 1996. The candidate has failed to satisfy the assessment criteria of applying relevant and accurate law to the client's case.
3. The candidate has correctly stated that Elizabeth can add Anna to the legal title but they then include irrelevant material relating to leaving a share in her will and cite s 14 Trusts of Land and Appointment of Trustees Act 1996 and *Sen v Headley* out of context. As before, this demonstrates a lack of care and precision.
4. It is not good practice to use secondary sources ahead of primary law or procedure. The candidate recognises that the article by Pawlowski is useful and relevant, but they should have quoted from the Law of Property Act 1925 first, as the primary source. The candidate also omits the second writer (Brown) when citing the article, which shows a lack of attention to detail. Furthermore, the candidate has misunderstood the sources or been careless when they say that the youngest tenant would be expected 'to die first in normal circumstances'; this contradicts the article and the statute, which hold that the youngest tenant would be expected to die *last*. Remember to review your answer carefully to pick up on this kind of mistake.
5. The candidate cites the ages of the two sisters incorrectly, which demonstrates ineffective use of the assessment material. This error has a profoundly damaging effect on the candidate's advice as it would directly affect the client in the event of simultaneous death, according to the doctrine of survivorship, as we see in the next paragraph.
6. The '*commorientes*' rule is the key to answering this question, and the candidate has done well to find the rule in the materials supplied and cite the relevant section: s 184 LPA 1925. Unfortunately, they have failed to apply it accurately to the facts because of errors in the previous paragraphs (misunderstanding the order of seniority in point 4 and also confusing the ages of the sisters in point 5).
7. It is always good practice and effective advice to find and explain any exceptions to rules of law and procedure, and the rebuttal of the presumption of *commorientes* is an important factor for this case but is missed entirely by the candidate. Also, the case of *Scarle v Scarle* is cited but used incorrectly in relation to the issue of 'order' - that was not the point in *Scarle* and this has been misunderstood.

Does this answer meet the threshold?

When assessing the second response against the SQE2 legal research assessment criteria, it is unlikely that it would meet the threshold standard. Although some correct sources were selected, the candidate has misinterpreted the law and cited other irrelevant sources too. They made inaccurate assumptions about case law and errors in extracting the correct information from the question, so the advice fails to be client-focused. The candidate has not applied the law correctly or comprehensively to the client's situation, and the advice was not precise or clear. The answer was also too brief and does not show full understanding.

SQE2 can assess any of the areas on the SQE1 wills and estates specification. Below is an example of how a different part of the specification could arise in the context of SQE2 legal research. This time, the issue is on the challenging area of secret trusts. These are not on the FLK syllabus but, as they appear on the face of a will, this topic falls within the general ambit of wills and estates.

■ QUESTION 2

Email to candidate

From: Partner
Sent: 13 May 202#
To: Candidate
Subject: Jordan Waxford (deceased)

Last week we were instructed by Nick Blair in relation to his late employer Jordan's estate. It seems that Jordan died unexpectedly, but not before communicating key information and instructions to Nick.

Nick was Jordan's driver, and gave us the following information. Jordan was married but had been having an affair with Sam for several years and intended to file for divorce. There was an addendum to Jordan's original will that mentions that Nick is to be the 'beneficiary' of the sum of £100,000, and there was no mention in the will of Sam. Nick says that, before the addendum was executed formally, he accepted a sealed envelope containing a letter from Jordan only to be opened in the event of Jordan dying. Nick did not know the contents of the letter but did not directly refuse to carry out Jordan's wishes. He has now opened the letter, which contains details of what he was to do with the £100,000, namely to pass it over to Sam. In effect it seems that Nick was not the true beneficiary, as the will states that Jordan gives '£100,000 to my good friend Nick in order that he will follow my instructions'.

Please could you research this matter for me and discover whether:
- **Nick is likely to be bound by the instructions in the envelope.**
- **Sam may be able to benefit if they are not referred to in the will.**

I would like you to include, for my reference, your legal reasoning, mentioning any key sources or authorities.

Many thanks

Partner

Note to candidates:

Given the time constraints of this assessment, we have not provided the full text of some primary sources. Where the full text of a primary source is not provided, candidates may nevertheless cite the primary source on the basis it is referred to in one or more of the secondary sources provided and the full text can be checked at a later date.

Information displayed is as obtained on the date of search, for example purposes only. Information herein is not to be relied upon outside the purposes of this sample question.

Attachments

You have been provided with the following sources listed alphabetically in order of source name. The order of presentation is not intended as a guide to the order in which they should be consulted.

PLEASE NOTE THAT PART OR ALL OF SOME OF THESE SOURCES MAY NOT BE RELEVANT TO ANSWERING THE QUESTION

1. *Blackwell v Blackwell* [1929] UKHL 1
2. 'Certainty of Intention and the Creation of Secret Trusts in a Recent Case' (March 2021) Owen Curry, XXIV Old Buildings, *Private Legal Update* no. 19, https://xxiv.co.uk/certainty-of-intention-and-the-creation-of-secret-trusts-in-a-recent-case/
3. *Halsbury's Laws of England*, Wills and Intestacy, vol. 102 para. 222
4. *Halsbury's Laws of England*, Trusts and Powers, vol. 98 para. 35
5. *Rawstron & Anor (Executrices of the Estate of Lucian Freud) v Freud* [2014] EWHC 2577 Ch
6. Wills Act 1837 c 26 ss 1, 3, 9, 15, 17, 20, 21
7. 'Wills and Undue Influence: Lessons from Rea v Rea' (2024), Hamed Ovaisi, SO Legal, www.solegal.co.uk/insights/wills-and-undue-influence-lessons-rea-v-rea-2024

* * *

Source 1

Blackwell v Blackwell [1929] UKHL 1

LORD BUCKMASTER:

The LORD CHANCELLOR desires me to say that he agrees with this opinion that I am about to read. The question raised on this appeal is one which in various forms has for over two hundred years been the subject of vexed controversy. It may be stated by asking to what extent is it possible to give effect to testamentary intentions that are at variance with the provisions first of the Statute of Frauds and later of the Wills Act. That some deviation from the strict letter of these statutes has been permitted and has now become settled law is not disputed.

If a testator in his will makes a gift to a named legatee who at the time of making the will has promised he will hold the benefit of the gift for certain defined and lawful purposes, the Court will enforce against the legatee the trust in promised obedience to which he received the gift. (McCormick v Grogan 4 E. & I. Appeals 82.)

This, however, does not directly govern the present case as the following facts will show. The Testator at the time of his death had a son of 16 years, the child of a woman, also living, who was not his wife. He was ill for many weeks before he died and was much concerned as to how he should make provision for this woman and her child without disclosing all the circumstances in his will. [. . .]

I omit the detailed examination of other cases for they are all carefully considered and dealt with by Hall, V-C., in the case of In re Fleetwood (15 Chancery Division; 594), an authority which indisputably covers the present case if it be accurately decided. In that case the testatrix left to a named person all her personalty, 'to be applied as I have requested him to do.' The request was made out and the named trustee jotted down in the presence of the testatrix the names of the persons and the amounts which the testatrix desired to give and, after this, the codicil was executed. The point raised was the same as in the present case, viz., that when the trusteeship appears upon the instrument the trust must be for the next-of-kin or residuary legatees and that the Wills Act prevented effect being given to a trust to be effected by parol evidence. The learned Vice-Chancellor went through all the cases, including the case of McCormick v. Grogan, and decided that the trusts should be executed. [. . .]

Viscount Sumner.

MY LORDS,

I am satisfied that in re Fleetwood, which is not distinguishable from the present case on the facts, was affirmed by the Court of Appeal in *In re Huxtable* and that professional opinion generally has accepted these decisions as correct. In argument, however, counsel for the Appellants treated it as almost self-evident that they conflicted with Section 9 of the Wills Act, and counsel for the Respondents, while making no admission, elected to rely mainly on the time that has passed and the probable volume of rights that have arisen, since these cases were decided, and in consequence of them. I do not think that this question ought to turn merely on the dates of the decisions and the extent of their adoption in practice. It is a grave thing to affirm a doctrine that violates the prescriptions of a statute and especially such a statute as the Wills Act, even though the error is of long standing. In view of this, and also in deference to the reservations of opinion expressed by Lords Dunedin and Parker of Waddington in *Lepage v. Gardom* (84 L.J. Ch. p. 749) and Lord Warrington of Clyffe in Gardner's Case (1920, 2 Ch. p. 532) I venture to examine this aspect of the matter.

In itself the doctrine of equity, by which parol evidence is admissible to prove what is called 'fraud' in connexion with secret trusts, and effect is given to such trusts when established, would not seem to conflict with any of the Acts under which from time to time the Legislature has regulated the right of testamentary disposition. A Court of conscience finds a man in the position of an absolute legal owner of a sum of money, which has been bequeathed to him under a valid will, and it declares that, on proof of certain facts relating to the motives and actions of the testator, it will not allow the legal owner to exercise his legal right to do what he will with his own. This seems to be a perfectly normal exercise of general equitable jurisdiction. The facts commonly but not necessarily involve some immoral and selfish conduct on the part of the legal owner. The necessary elements, on which the question turns are intention, communication, and acquiescence. The testator intends his absolute gift to be employed as he and not as the donee desires; he tells the proposed donee of this intention and, either by express promise or by the tacit promise, which is signified by acquiescence, the proposed donee encourages him to bequeath the money in the faith that his intentions will be carried out. The special circumstance, that the gift is by bequest, only makes this rule a special case of the exercise of a general jurisdiction, but in its application to a bequest the doctrine must in principle rest on the assumption that the will has first operated according to its terms. It is because there is no one, to whom the law can give relief in the premises, that relief, if any, must be sought in equity. So far, and in the bare case of a legacy absolute on the face of it, I do not see how the statute-law relating to the form of a valid will is concerned at all, and the expressions in which the doctrine has been habitually described seem to bear this out. For the prevention of fraud equity fastens on the conscience of the legatee a trust, a trust, that is, which otherwise would be inoperative; in other words it makes him do what the will in itself has nothing to do with; it lets him take what the will gives him and: then makes him apply it, as the Court of conscience directs, and it does so in order to give effect to wishes of the testator, which would not otherwise be effectual.

To this two circumstances must be added to bring the present case to the test of the general doctrine, first, that the will states on its face that the legacy is given on trust but does not state what the trusts are, and further contains a residuary bequest, and, second, that the legatees are acting with perfect honesty, seek no advantage to themselves, and only desire, if the Court will permit them, to do what in other circumstances the Court would have fastened it on their conscience to perform.

* * *

Source 2

'Certainty of Intention and the Creation of Secret Trusts in a Recent Case' (March 2021) Owen Curry, XXIV Old Buildings, *Private Legal Update* no. 19, https://xxiv.co.uk/certainty-of-intention-and-the-creation-of-secret-trusts-in-a-recent-case/

Introduction to secret trusts

The doctrine of secret trusts is an example of one of those by-ways of English equity jurisprudence that throws up a factually interesting case from time to time.

Secret trusts come in two types: half secret trusts and fully secret trusts. In the case of a half secret trust the existence of the trust is apparent from the will but the beneficial interests are not set out. In the case of a fully secret trust, the will appears to contain an outright gift to the (secret) trustee.

There are three requirements for a secret trust: (1) intention to create the trust; (2) communication of the trust to the trustee (which is subject to slightly different rules on timing depending on whether the trust is half-secret or fully secret) and (3) acceptance of the trust by the trustee.

It is possible for secret and half secret trusts to be created with reasonable formality – with the trusts properly set out in writing in some, private, document outside (or *dehors* in the old language found in some cases) the will. A recent example of this was the estate of the painter Lucian Freud: *Re Freud* [2014] EWHC 2577 in which the claimant executors who were beneficially entitled to the whole residuary estate on the face of the will made clear that they had received the estate subject to a fully secret trust.

Inevitably, however, secret trusts often arise, or are alleged to arise, where the terms of the trust have not been committed to writing in full or at all. A secret trust need not be set out in writing: *Ottaway v Norman* [1972] Ch 698. And where the trust alleged has been created informally, a central issue for the Court will often be whether the testator actually intended to create a trust at all.

Ms Richards' jewellery

In *Titcombe v Ison* (ChD, 28th January 2021), unreported, the Court had to consider whether a valuable collection of jewellery was subject to a secret trust. The jewellery had belonged to one Ms Richards. She had no children and, on her death, left her whole estate to her friend, Mr Ison. Her niece, Mrs Titcombe, brought a claim for jewellery on the basis that Mr Ison had agreed with Ms Richards that, after her death, he would give the jewellery to the claimant. She claimed that as a result Mr Ison now held the jewellery on a bare (secret) trust for her.

The three certainties

Like any other trust a secret trust must satisfy the three certainties: intention, subject matter, and objects. In *Titcombe v Ison* the key issue was whether Ms Richards had intended to create a trust.

Mr Ison did not dispute that Ms Richards had had some wishes and intentions regarding the jewellery - including that some be given to the claimant and that he had agreed and wished to respect her wishes. But he denied that she had intended to create a bare trust in the claimant's favour.

Deputy Master Rhys was assisted in deciding this point by the comments in two cases.

First in *Kasperbauer v Griffiths* [2000] WTLR 333 the Court of Appeal had summarised the law in this area and pointed out that the question was whether the testator intended a trust or '*a mere moral or family obligation.*'

Second, the older case of *McCormick v Grogan* (1867) I LR Eq 313, (1869) LR App 82 which was a decision of the Irish Court of Appeal upheld by the House of Lords. In that case the Court was dealing with a trust allegedly created by a letter giving directions regarding the testator's property in which the testator had requested that his friend deal with the property as the testator would have done had he been alive. The Court asked whether the testator could have intended the wishes expressed in the letter to be the subject of a legal sanction if not followed.

Deputy Master Rhys adopted this approach. He directed himself '*In determining a claim to a secret trust, therefore, the court must determine whether the wishes of the testator were intended to create a trust, or simply "a mere moral or family obligation?" In reaching that decision, it is necessary to ascertain what sanction the testator intended for compliance with his wishes. If the intended sanction was the authority of the court, a trust is created. If the matter was left simply to the conscience of the donee, then there is no trust but a moral obligation.*'

Conclusion

In *Titcombe v Ison* there was no doubt that the testator had expressed informal wishes regarding her jewellery. But the manner in which those wishes had been expressed and the fact that Ms Richards' wishes were not (as the Court found) for the Claimant to be the sole recipient of her jewellery, led to the conclusion that the answer to the question 'had Ms Richards intended her wishes to be sanctioned by the authority of the court?' was: no. Accordingly no trust was created.

* * *

Source 3

Reproduced by permission of RELX (UK) Limited, trading as LexisNexis.

Halsbury's Laws of England > Wills and Intestacy (Volume 102 (2016), paras 1–564; Volume 103 (2016), paras 565–1301) > 4. Construction of Wills > (2) Admissibility of Evidence > (iv) Evidence of Secret Trusts > 222. Fully secret trusts

Para 222

Where on the face of the will the gift is an absolute one [. . .], but it can be proved [. . .] that either before [. . .] or after [. . .] the date of the will, but during the testator's lifetime [. . .], the donee received from the testator a communication of certain **trusts** or conditions to be attached to the gift[6] and to be binding on the donee [. . .], and that the donee accepted the gift on those **trusts** and conditions, either by his express agreement or by his silence[8], and thereby induced the testator to make the gift, or to leave the gift already made unrevoked, then evidence of those **trusts** or conditions may be admissible, except in so far as such evidence would contradict the will [. . .]

---

[6] The method by which the testator's intentions are to be carried out is not material: see *Ottaway v Norman* [1972] Ch 698, [1971] 3 All ER 1325 [. . .]

[8] The acceptance may be made expressly or silently, as where the donee does not dissent on the communication being made to him: see *Russell v Jackson* (1852) 10 Hare 204; *Moss v Cooper* (1861) 1 John & H 352 at 370–371 [. . .]

* * *

Source 4

Reproduced by permission of RELX (UK) Limited, trading as LexisNexis.

Halsbury's Laws of England > Trusts and Powers (Volume 98 (2019)) > 1. Nature and Creation of Trusts and Powers > (1) Introduction > (iii) Classification of Trusts > 35. Secret trusts

Para 35

A secret trust is created where property is in law given to a person either absolutely or upon an indefinite trust, but there has been an undertaking by him or an understanding between him and the donor, not clothed with the requisite formalities for the creation of a lawful trust, that it is to be applied for the benefit of some other person or object[1]. There must be evidence that the testator intended to impose a legally enforceable duty and not merely a moral obligation[2].

---

[1] *McCormick v Grogan* (1869) LR 4 HL 82 at 88–89 per Lord Hatherley LC; *Re Stead, Witham v Andrew* [1900] 1 Ch 237 at 240–241, CA, per Farwell J. [. . .]

[2] *Kasperbauer v Griffiths* [2002] WTLR 333, CA [. . .]

* * *

Source 5

Rawstron & Anor (Executrices of the Estate of Lucian Freud) v Freud [2014] EWHC 2577 Ch

16. Turning from principles of interpretation to the difference between fully secret and half secret trusts, *Theobald on Wills*, 17th edn, states at paragraphs 6-001, 6-004 and 6-009:

> 'secret trusts provide for the testator a means of creating a trust without publicly identifying the beneficiary and/or the terms of the trust. A trust is fully secret if the will does not disclose that the trust exists, and half secret if the will discloses that there is a trust but does not disclose the objects and/or terms of the trust.'
>
> 'In the case of a fully secret trust, it is immaterial whether the trust is communicated and accepted before or after execution of the will[.] Nevertheless, communication must occur in the testator's lifetime, otherwise it cannot be enforced and the legatee will take beneficially.'
>
> 'A half secret trust will fail if the details are not communicated to the trustee until after the execution of the will. There is thus a distinction between a fully secret trust, where the trust can be communicated at any time before the testator's death; and a half secret trust, where the trust must be communicated before or contemporaneously with the will.'

17. The statements in *Williams on Wills*, 9th edn, at paragraphs 36.1, 36.4-36.5 and 36.10-36.11 are to the same effect:

> 'There are two kinds of secret trusts in common use. In the first the property is given to the apparent beneficiary for an absolute interest though he secretly acquiesces with the testator that he will hold it on certain trusts. The other class is where in the will the apparent beneficiary is by the terms of the will a mere trustee but the nature of the trusts upon which he is to hold the property are not disclosed or not fully disclosed.'
>
> 'The [fully secret] trusts but not the gift itself will fail where the intended trust, though not void in law, is not communicated to the donee in the lifetime of the testator[.] Where the trust fails because it is not communicated to the donee the donee takes the gift absolutely and free of trust.'
>
> 'Where the property is given by will to persons upon trusts which are referred to in, but not defined by, the will, the trustees cannot take beneficially and the trustees hold the property either for the secret beneficiaries or, if the trusts fail, for those entitled to residue or on intestacy as the case may be[.] If the beneficial trusts are defined and communicated to the trustees on or before the execution of the will, the trusts are unenforceable, as being an attempt to empower the testator to make unwitnessed dispositions by naming trustees and leaving the details of the trusts to be supplied afterwards.'

* * *

Source 6

Wills Act 1837 c 26 ss 1, 3, 9, 15, 17, 20, 21

[1.] Meaning of certain words in this Act: 'Will': 'Real estate': 'Personal estate': Number: Gender

The words and expressions herein-after mentioned, which in their ordinary signification have a more confined or a different meaning, shall in this Act, except where the nature of the provision or the context of the Act shall exclude such construction, be interpreted as follows; (that is to say,) the word 'will' shall extend to a testament, and to a codicil, and to an appointment by will or by writing in the nature of a will in exercise of a power, **[F2** and also to an appointment by will of a guardian of a child,**] [F1** and also to an appointment by will of a representative under section 4 of the Human Tissue Act 2004**] [F3** or section 8 of the Human Transplantation (Wales) Act 2013], [. . .] **F4** and to any other testamentary disposition; and the words 'real estate' shall extend to manors, advowsons, messuages, lands, tithes, rents, and hereditaments, [. . .] **F4** whether corporeal, incorporeal, or personal, **[F5** and to any undivided share thereof,] and to any estate, right, or interest (other than a chattel interest) therein; and the words 'personal estate' shall extend to leasehold estates and other chattels real, and also to monies, shares of government and other funds, securities for money (not being real estates), debts, choses in action, rights, credits, goods, and all other property whatsoever which by law devolves upon the executor or administrator, and to any share or interest therein; and every word importing the singular number only shall extend and be applied to several persons or things as well as one person or thing; and every word importing the masculine gender only shall extend and be applied to a female as well as a male.

Textual amendments

F1 Words in s. 1 inserted (20.10.2005 for specified purposes, 1.9.2006 in so far as not already in force) by Human Tissue Act 2004 (c. 30), s. 60(2), Sch. 6 para. 1 (with s. 58); S.I. 2005/2792, art. 2(2)(j); S.I. 2006/1997, art. 3(2) (with arts. 4 7 8) (as amended (5.8.2006) by S.I. 2006/2169, art. 2)

F2 Words substituted by Children Act 1989 (c. 41, SIF 20), s. 108(5)(6), Sch. 13 para. 1: S.I. 1991/828, art. 3(2) (with Sch. 14 para. 1(1))

F3 Words in s. 1 inserted (1.12.2015) by Human Transplantation (Wales) Act 2013 (anaw 5), ss. 17, 21(1) (with s. 14); S.I. 2015/1679, art. 3(e)

F4 Words repealed by Statute Law (Repeals) Act 1969 (c. 52), Sch. Pt. III

F5 Words in s. 1 repealed (E.W.) (1.1.1997) by 1996 c. 47, s. 25(2), Sch. 4 (with ss. 24(2), 25(4)(5)); S.I. 1996/2974, art. 2

3 All property may be disposed of by will; Contingent Interests; Rights of Entry; and property acquired after the execution of the will

It shall be lawful for every person to devise, bequeath, or dispose of, by his will executed in manner herein-after required, all real estate and all personal estate which he shall be entitled to, either at law or in equity, at the time of his death, and which, if not so devised, bequeathed, or disposed of, would devolve [. . .] **F1** upon his executor or administrator; and the power hereby given shall extend [. . .] **F1** to all contingent, executory or other future interests in any real or personal estate, whether the testator may or may not be ascertained as the person or one of the persons in whom the same respectively may become vested, and whether he may be entitled thereto under the instrument by which the same respectively were created, or under any disposition thereof by deed or will; and also to all rights of entry for conditions broken, and other rights of entry; and also to such of the same estates, interests, and rights respectively, and other real and personal estate, as the testator may be entitled to at the time of his death, notwithstanding that he may become entitled to the same subsequently to the execution of his will.

Textual amendments

F1 Words repealed by Statute Law (Repeals) Act 1969 (c. 52), Sch. Pt. III

[F1 9 Signing and attestation of wills

[F2 (1)**]** No will shall be valid unless—

(a) it is in writing, and signed by the testator, or by some other person in his presence and by his direction; and
(b) it appears that the testator intended by his signature to give effect to the will; and
(c) the signature is made or acknowledged by the testator in the presence of two or more witnesses present at the same time; and
(d) each witness either—
   (i) attests and signs the will; or
   (ii) acknowledges his signature,
   in the presence of the testator (but not necessarily in the presence of any other witness),

but no form of attestation shall be necessary.

[F3 (2) For the purposes of paragraphs (c) and (d) of subsection (1), in relation to wills made on or after 31 January 2020 and on or before 31 January **[F4** 2024**]**, 'presence' includes presence by means of videoconference or other visual transmission.**]]**

Textual Amendments

F1 S. 9 substituted by Administration of Justice Act 1982 (c. 53, SIF 116:5), ss. 17, 73(6)

F2 S. 9 renumbered as s. 9(1) (28.9.2020) by virtue of The Wills Act 1837 (Electronic Communications) (Amendment) (Coronavirus) Order 2020 (S.I. 2020/952), arts. 1, 2(2) (with art. 3)

F3 S. 9(2) inserted (28.9.2020) by The Wills Act 1837 (Electronic Communications) (Amendment) (Coronavirus) Order 2020 (S.I. 2020/952), arts. 1, 2(3) (with art. 3)

F4 Word in s. 9(2) substituted (1.2.2022) by The Wills Act 1837 (Electronic Communications) (Amendment) Order 2022 (S.I. 2022/18), arts. 1, 2(2)

15 Gifts to an attesting witness to be void

If any person shall attest the execution of any will to whom or to whose wife or husband any beneficial devise, legacy, estate, interest, gift, or appointment, of or affecting any real or personal estate (other than and except charges and directions for the payment of any debt or debts), shall be thereby given or made, such devise, legacy, estate, interest, gift, or appointment shall, so far only as concerns such person attesting the execution of such will, or the wife or husband of such person, or any person claiming under such person or wife or husband, be utterly null and void, and such person so attesting shall be admitted as a witness to prove the execution of such will, or to prove the validity or invalidity thereof, notwithstanding such devise, legacy, estate, interest, gift, or appointment mentioned in such will.

17 Executor shall be admitted a witness

No person shall, on account of his being an executor of a will, be incompetent to be admitted a witness to prove the execution of such will, or a witness to prove the validity or invalidity thereof.

20 No will to be revoked but by another will or codicil, or by a writing executed like a will, or by destruction

No will or codicil, or any part thereof, shall be revoked otherwise than as aforesaid, or by another will or codicil executed in manner herein-before required, or by some writing declaring an intention to revoke the same, and executed in the manner in which a will is herein-before required to be executed, or by the burning, tearing, or otherwise destroying the same by the testator, or by some person in his presence and by his direction, with the intention of revoking the same.

21 No alteration in a will shall have any effect unless executed as a will

No obliteration, interlineation, or other alteration made in any will after the execution thereof shall be valid or have any effect, except so far as the words or effect of the will before such alteration shall not be apparent, unless such alteration shall be executed in like manner as herein-before is required for the execution of the will; but the will, with such alteration as part thereof, shall be deemed to be duly executed if the signature of the testator and the subscription of the witnesses be made in the margin or on some other part of the will opposite or near to such alteration, or at the foot or end of or opposite to a memorandum referring to such alteration, and written at the end or some other part of the will.

* * *

Source 7

'Wills and Undue Influence: Lessons from Rea v Rea' (2024), Hamed Ovaisi, SO Legal, www.solegal.co.uk/insights/wills-and-undue-influence-lessons-rea-v-rea-2024

The Court of Appeal recently handed down judgment in Rea v Rea, a long-running family dispute over the validity of a will. The case is a timely reminder of the difference between persuasion and coercion.

Several weeks after the ruling judgment of Rea v Rea (2024), our litigation team reflects on its importance in establishing testamentary undue influence.

Requirements to create a will

In order to create a will, a testator (i.e. the person creating a will) must satisfy several requirements, which may vary depending on the contents of the will, the types of assets being transferred or gifted, and the potential complexities in creating a trust.

At a very basic level, a will must be correctly executed by the testator and be witnessed by two independent individuals who are present together at the time of signing. Where a will is gifting or transferring property, it must also be executed as a deed. As for the contents of the will, it must be possible to identify the property being transferred or gifted, as well as each individual beneficiary's interest in the property.

Potentially, the most important requirement to evidence when creating a will, however, is being able to ascertain the true intention of the testator. Did they mean to create a will and if so, do the terms reflect their intentions? It is therefore critical to consider a testator's words and conduct in the creation of their will, as well as the express terms of that will when assessing its validity.

The importance of assessing the intentions of a testator was recently evaluated in the landmark judgment of Rea v Rea (2024), where three sons of a testator challenged the validity of their mother's will, claiming she had been unduly influenced by their sister, who had taken unfair advantage of her position and coerced their mother into creating a new will which excluded them from jointly inheriting her most valuable asset, her £1m house in London.

Undue influence

Undue influence is a legal protection afforded to those who can prove that a person has taken unfair advantage of their position by abusing their influence over another. The concept of undue influence originates back to the nineteenth century and has gradually developed from the principle of duress, which originally sought to restrict the influence of physical coercion.

Undue influence, on the other hand, is more subtle in that it seeks to restrict the influence of non-physical coercion. The assessment of what does or does not constitute coercion in contrast to persuasion has been a focal issue for the court over the years, and it is within this grey area that the merits of an Undue Influence claim will succeed or fail. [. . .]

In scenarios where undue influence is established, an applicant must prove that an unwarranted pressure has overpowered the testator's own volition. As summarised in the case of Wingrove v Wingrove (1885) '*It is only when the will of the person who becomes a testator is coerced into doing that which he or she does not desire to do [. . .] that is undue influence*'.

Contesting the validity of a will on account of the terms not reflecting a testator's intentions can be extremely difficult for an applicant for several reasons.

Firstly, there is usually no direct evidence to demonstrate the actual coercion that may have influenced the testator. This point was notably summarised in Schrader v Schrader (2013): '*It will be a common feature of a large number of undue influence cases that there is no direct evidence of the application of influence. It is of the nature of undue influence that it goes when no-one is looking. That does not stop its being proved. The proof has to come, if at all from more circumstantial evidence.*'

The weight and severity of circumstantial evidence can vary, however, and depending on the context surrounding the testator, certain forms of pressure, which in one circumstance may amount to coercion, may not in another.

This subjective issue was further raised in the case of Wingrove v Wingrove (1885): 'it may be in the grossest form, such as actual confinement or violence, or a person in the days or hours of life may become so weak and feeble, that a very little pressure will be sufficient to bring about the desired result, and it may even be, that the mere talking to him at that stage of illness and pressing something upon him may so fatigue the brain that the sick person may be induced, for quietness' sake, to do anything'.

Lastly, and quite possibly the most controversial, in order to satisfy the requirements to establish undue influence, it must be shown that the only hypothesis which is consistent with the facts is that the testator was coerced into creating the will. As affirmed by Lord Cranworth LC in Boyse v Rossborough (1857), '*it is not sufficient to show that the circumstances attending its execution are consistent with the hypothesis of its having been obtained by undue influence. It must be shown that they are inconsistent with a contrary hypothesis*'.

Undue influence is, therefore, a difficult protection to rely on. The burden of proof for establishing testamentary undue influence lies with the party seeking to disprove the validity of a will. They must demonstrate that on the balance of probabilities it was more likely than not that the testator was coerced into writing (or rewriting) the will.

With scenarios differing on the most subtle of differences, there is often a disparity of opinions and interpretations from judges, as seen in the contrasting judgments of Rea v Rea (2019), Rea v Rea (2023) and Rea v Rea (2024).

Background to Rea v Rea

Anna Rea, the testator in proceedings, died in 2016, naming her four children, Rita (the claimant), Remo, Nino and David (the defendants) as the beneficiaries in her will. Although Anna originally signed a simple one-page will in 1986, in 2015 she executed a new will, gifting her most substantial asset, her house in south London, to Rita as opposed to the terms of the 1986 will, which declared her estate to be equally divided between her four children.

Anna had suffered from several health issues during the last 20 years of her life. In light of Anna's disabilities, Rita moved in with her mother in 2009 to act as her carer. Anna's respective relationships with three of her children, namely, Remo, Nino and David deteriorated between 2009 and 2015 on account of their unwillingness to support or contribute to their mother's care. Anna's frustration was duly recorded in her 2015 will, where she affirmed:

> *'I DECLARE that my sons do not help with my care and there have been numerous calls for help from me, but they are not engaging with any help or assistance. My sons have not taken care of me and my daughter Rita Rea has been my sole*

carer for many years. Hence should any of my sons challenge my estate I wish my executors to defend any such claim as they are not dependent on me, and I do not wish for them to share in my estate save what I have stated in this will.'

Crucially, the 2015 will was drafted by a specialist solicitor who was a member of two highly regarded associations, and the 2015 will was similarly witnessed by Anna's longstanding GP.

2019 – Trial

[. . .] Following a three-day trial in September 2019, the judge considered several pieces of evidence, including Anna's GP's attendance note (evaluating her capacity), as well as the GP's oral submissions, and concluded that Remo, Nino and David's undue influence counterclaim had fallen well short of the requirements needed to succeed. Accordingly, the judged ruled in Rita's favour and gave instructions for the 2015 will to be admitted to probate.

Although the three brothers' initial appeal was rejected in 2021, their subsequent appeal was granted in 2022 when the court acknowledged that a procedural error had '*caused serious prejudice*' in that the defendant's counsel was unable to cross-examine Rita on several issues. A retrial was, therefore, scheduled for 2023.

2023 – High Court Decision

The matter was readmitted to the High Court, with the matter coming before the High Court in July 2023. Upon reviewing the evidence, the High Court judge reversed the previous ruling, stating that although at first sight, it may seem a surprising conclusion given the GP and solicitor's involvement in creating the 2015 will, they were nevertheless satisfied that '*the facts are consistent only with Rita having procured the making and execution of the 2015 will by the exercise of undue influence over her mother*'. [. . .]

2024 – Court of Appeal Decision

On 1 February 2024, the matter was heard by the Court of Appeal. Upon reviewing the evidence, on 23 February 2024 the final judgment was handed down by the three judges, who confirmed that the test for undue influence was not met, and Rita was therefore successful in her claim. [. . .]

Conclusions

The case of Rea v Rea is a stark reminder that in order to satisfy the considerably high bar in establishing undue influence, parties must ensure that the evidence put forward is only consistent with the hypothesis that a testator was coerced into creating a will.

Although either side may provide conflicting narratives to support or disprove circumstantial evidence, to succeed in establishing undue influence, a party must demonstrate that it was more likely than not that a testator was coerced and not persuaded.

The subtle difficulty in reviewing evidence of this kind and demonstrating that the facts are or are not consistent with this test is considerably nuanced and requires expert support.

* * *

■ YOUR TURN

Have a go at answering question 2, remembering the guidance on pages 24–26.

- Remember the structured approach in the SRA's assessment criteria on page 25.
- Make a list of the relevant answers to the legal points raised in your instructions and addressed in the sources, remembering to use primary sources over secondary sources wherever possible.
- Evaluate the sources, and remember that some of them may not be relevant to your answer.
- Timings are important: you will need to prepare and write your answer in one hour.

SQE1 Functioning legal knowledge link

Remember from ***Revise SQE: Wills and Administration of Estates***, chapter 1, that wills must generally follow the rules relating to formalities; chapter 11 also states that there are rules as to the duties of trustees where property appears to be held on trust for beneficiaries. Secret trusts are generally found 'hidden' inside a will, with further instructions provided outside the will itself.

EVALUATING YOUR ANSWER

When you have attempted question 2, mark it yourself against the SQE2 legal research assessment criteria. Do you think your attempt met the threshold standard?

Now compare your attempt with the following key legal points and two sample answers to question 2. A circled number indicates that commentary is provided for this part of the answer. The commentary explains whether or not the sample satisfies the assessment criteria, and accordingly whether it is likely to meet the SQE2 threshold standard.

➥Key legal points: question 2

In this assessment, part, or all, of the following sources are relevant to the question:

- *Blackwell v Blackwell* [1929] UKHL 1
- 'Certainty of Intention and the Creation of Secret Trusts in a Recent Case' (March 2021) Owen Curry, XXIV Old Buildings, *Private Legal Update* no. 19, https://xxiv.co.uk/certainty-of-intention-and-the-creation-of-secret-trusts-in-a-recent-case/
- *Halsbury's Laws of England*, Wills and Intestacy, vol. 102 para. 222
- *Halsbury's Laws of England*, Trusts and Powers, vol. 98 para. 35
- *Rawstron & Anor (Executrices of the Estate of Lucian Freud) v Freud* [2014] EWHC 2577 Ch
- Wills Act 1837 c 26 ss 9 and 15

The following source is not relevant to the question:

- 'Wills and Undue Influence: Lessons from Rea v Rea' (2024), Hamed Ovaisi, SO Legal, www.solegal.co.uk/insights/wills-and-undue-influence-lessons-rea-v-rea-2024

Key legal points include the following:

- Ordinarily, if Jordan has died leaving a will, then any general, specific or demonstrative legacies can take effect provided the formalities are present (s 9 Wills Act 1837).
- If the will states that £100,000 is to go to Nick, then, provided that Nick has not witnessed and signed the will, Nick can benefit from the pecuniary legacy (s 15 Wills Act 1837).

- However, it seems that a letter was handed to Nick before the addendum was executed, with instructions to hand the £100,000 to Sam. This does not appear anywhere in the will itself. This then invokes the rules of so-called secret trusts, as there are instructions given to Nick on what to do with the money.
- According to *Kasperbauer*, cited in Curry's 'Certainty of Intention' article, secret trusts are valid if, to begin with, the three certainties under the law of equity and trusts are present: intention, subject matter and objects. These certainties seem to be clear on the facts of this case.
- The difference between a fully secret trust and a half-secret trust is explained in Curry's article and also in *Rawstron & Anor (Executrices of the Estate of Lucian Freud) v Freud* [2014]. Secret trusts fall into two categories – full and half. Full is where the will makes no reference to any other beneficiary or legatee, and half is where the will refers to a beneficiary or legatee but does not name them. Here, as the will has a pecuniary legacy for Nick but includes 'in order that he will follow my instructions', this is therefore a half-secret trust that has words pointing to a secondary beneficiary (however that may be implied).
- For a half-secret trust to be valid, there must be communication of the trust before the will, addendum or codicil is executed and also accepted by Nick. *Ottaway v Norman* 1972 as cited in *Halsbury's Laws of England*, Wills and Intestacy (vol. 102, para. 222) states that 'the method by which the testator's intentions are to be carried out is not material', and Curry confirms that the intentions do not need to be written down. If Nick does not clearly say 'no', the half-secret trust is valid and Nick is bound by the contents of the letter (even in a sealed envelope) providing the instructions within are clear and relate to the property being given to the secret beneficiary.
- This seems to be the case, and, providing Nick does not revoke before Jordan's death, the secret trust is valid and Sam takes beneficially (*Blackwell v Blackwell* [1929]). This is true even if Sam witnesses and signs the will, because a secret beneficiary takes from the trust and not the will – the dehors the will theory (Curry's article).
- Note that the article on 'Wills and Undue Influence' is not relevant here. The question poses issues as to secret trusts, and there is no element of undue influence.
- Remember that the question is only requiring research as to the issue of the secret trust, but FLK1 knowledge can be applied to fully understand the context of the question.

■ SAMPLE ANSWER 1 TO QUESTION 2

At common law, there are only two methods by which property is distributed after someone's death. The first one is distribution of property according to the testator's will. For this to happen, the deceased must have created a valid will that complies with s 9 of the Wills Act 1837. This requires a will to be in writing, signed by the testator, or by some other person who signs in his presence and by his direction, in the presence of two witnesses both present at the same time, who also sign. All dispositions must be clear and visible on the will. This does not seem to be an issue with Jordan's will, although it is not clear on the facts. ❶

The second method is by the intestacy rules, which are not relevant here. ❷

A secret trust arises when a testator makes a gift of property in his will to A (in this case to Nick) but with the intention that A holds the property on trust for B (in this case, for Sam). This is explained by Lord Buckmaster in *Blackwell v Blackwell* [1929] UKHL 1 and as cited in Owen Curry's article 'Certainty of Intention'.

However, either this intention is not clear on the face of the will at all (a fully secret trust) or the intention is clear but the name of the beneficiary has been withheld (a half-secret trust). This means that on the face of it, secret trusts seem to sit outside the principles of the Wills Act and should not really exist. They do however operate by way of an exception to the Wills Act (*Rawstron & Anor (Executrices of the Estate of Lucian Freud) v Freud* [2014] EWHC 2577 Ch). ❸

There are two types of secret trust:

- **Fully secret trusts** - a trust is fully secret when both the existence of the trust and its terms are concealed; such a trust therefore arises where the property that is the subject of the trust is, on the face of the will, left to the recipient absolutely (see Curry's article). This is not the case with Nick.
- **Half-secret trusts** - a trust is half secret when the existence of a trust is revealed but its terms are concealed; such a trust therefore arises where the property that is the subject matter of the trust is, on the face of the will, left to the recipient as a trustee. For example: '£100,000 to Nick so that he will do as I have instructed.' This is relevant here, so this is a half-secret trust.

In *both* cases, further explicit instructions must be communicated to the secret trustee (Nick) within the relevant timeframes. ❹

Requirements for a valid secret trust

The basic prerequisite for all secret trusts, from *Kasperbauer v Griffiths* as cited in Curry's article, is to set down a legally enforceable duty, not just impose a moral obligation. As such the three certainties of intention, subject matter and objects must still be present. To apply this to the case:

Intention: This intention can be seen either from the will itself or in the case of fully secret trust, from communications or details outside the will (as with the letter to Nick).

Communication: The intention to create a trust must be communicated to the trustee. It can be done expressly or via constructive communication (*Rawstron & Anor (Executrices of the Estate of Lucian Freud) v Freud* [2014] EWHC 2577 Ch). If communication is constructive (via a sealed envelope) the trustee needs to know that the intention is to create a trust but the details can be found out later. This is exactly what happened with Nick, and all terms must be communicated. ❺

Acceptance: Secret trusts need to be accepted by the secret trustee. Acceptance can be express or constructive - by silent acquiescence - *Ottaway v Norman* [1972] and *Moss v Cooper* (1861) cited in *Halsbury's Laws of England > Wills and Intestacy* (Volume 102 (2016), para 222). Acceptance can be revoked provided the revocation is communicated to the testator within a reasonable time before his or her death. Nick accepted (even by silence) the terms of the letter inside a sealed envelope given to him within the relevant timeframe (before the addendum) and as far as we know did not revoke his trusteeship. ❻

In answer to the question therefore, unless Nick revoked the trusteeship within a reasonable time before Jordan's death (and there is no reason to think he did so), Nick must hand over the £100,000 to Sam on the event of Jordan's death. ❼

COMMENTARY

❶ The candidate begins strongly by explaining the formalities of a will. This is vital to draw a distinction between legacies in a will and the operation of secret trusts. The reference to s 9 Wills Act is therefore appropriate and necessary, and in this paragraph the candidate demonstrates the skill of being able to successfully apply relevant law to the scenario, as required by the assessment criteria.

2 The candidate recognises that intestacy is not relevant. In the SQE2 assessment, make sure that you keep calm and do not throw down on paper all that you know on a topic, as this is not the correct approach. The candidate raises and discounts intestacy quickly; this is sound practice, demonstrating focus on the client and what exactly they need to know.

3 There is good reference to the law here but without going into too much detail. The language used is clear and concise, as required by the assessment criteria, and shows the candidate's solid understanding of the materials in the research bundle.

4 There is good application to the scenario. Not only does the candidate effectively explain the difference between fully and half-secret trusts but they manage to apply this skilfully to the wording in the will. Nick as our client should be able to understand this clearly as the candidate has used simple language to make their point.

5 The candidate has used the material effectively, especially the case law references and points of law. It is always good practice to use primary sources over secondary, and the candidate has managed to effectively find relevant case law from the materials. This again demonstrates the ability to use only relevant materials.

6 As above, relevant case law has been applied in context and accurately, in order to apply the law to Nick's silent acceptance. The candidate has also suggested that, unless Nick revoked before Jordan died, he is bound by the terms of the instructions.

7 Finally, the candidate ends the advice clearly and succinctly, making sure that their points are made so the client can clearly understand their position.

Does this answer meet the threshold?

The sample answer contains all of the information that the client requires and that the candidate has been asked to provide. It discusses the relevant legislation under the Wills Act 1837, especially s 9, relevant case law such as *Kasperbauer v Griffiths*, *Ottaway v Norman* and *Rawstron v Freud*, and comment from secondary sources such as *Halsbury's* and Curry. The candidate explains how these sources apply to the scenario and are pertinent to the client's circumstances, accurately explaining the application of secret trusts. The answer is clear, succinct and legally correct, and therefore likely to meet the threshold standard for SQE2 legal research.

Now consider the second sample answer to question 2.

■ SAMPLE ANSWER 2 TO QUESTION 2

Intestacy rules apply either when there is no will or when a will is invalid owing to a lack of formalities or other issues. Jordan has left a will, and it seems to have complied with the formality requirements at s 9 of the Wills Act 1837. It is likely that Jordan would have created this will in writing and signed it in the presence of two witnesses both present at the same time, who also sign. All dispositions must be clear and visible on the will. 1

The second method is by the intestacy rules, which are not relevant here as Jordan had the relevant mental capacity to execute his will. However, it could be made invalid if there was an element of undue influence as there seems to be a relationship of trust and confidence. 2

As there are instructions given to Nick, Jordan's driver it seems that a secret trust is in operation as soon as Jordan has given these instructions to Nick to make a gift of property in their will to Nick but with the intention that he holds the property on trust for Sam.

The real beneficiary seems to be Sam but the will states that it is for Nick with no mention of Sam so this would seem to be a fully secret trust. Once Nick has received instructions from Jordan, he must follow the instructions in the envelope. It does not matter if Nick does not know what is in the envelope at the time it was handed to him by Jordan. ❸

The fact that money was left to Nick suggests this is not a half-secret trust. Providing Nick has taken the instructions from Jordan, he is bound to hand the money to Sam. ❹

The secret trust is still a trust, and, according to Curry's article, there needs to be certainty of intention, subject matter and objects. It seems that the intention is clear from Jordan that a trust is required; this is demonstrated in the words used in the will, and the money and Sam are clearly stated. The communication of the trust can be seen in the contents of the envelope. As long as it is handed over before Jordan's death, communication is valid. ❺

Acceptance

Secret trusts need to be accepted by the secret trustee. Acceptance can be express or constructive, and as Nick has accepted the letter his acceptance is valid, but Nick can only revoke his acceptance at any time until the will is executed. ❻

Nick accepted the terms of the letter inside a sealed envelope given to him and had no intention of revoking his trusteeship. Nick must hand over the £100,000 to Sam on the event of Jordan's death. ❼

COMMENTARY

❶ This is not necessarily the best way to begin the answer: the candidate starts by explaining intestacy, which is not relevant, and then assumes that Jordan's will is valid but without evidence from the facts. This demonstrates a lack of application and focus on the needs of the client.

❷ Other errors are made here. First, although it is correct that intestacy does not apply, the candidate makes another assumption that Jordan was not lacking capacity. This is an example of extending the facts to make their point, which should never be done, either in the assessment or in practice. It is extremely important to analyse only the fact pattern provided in the instructions; not doing so is potentially a professional conduct issue. Second, the candidate has wrongly referred to undue influence as a way that the will could be invalidated. Though there may be a relationship of trust and confidence here, there is no evidence of any such undue influence as no improper pressure was applied by Jordan on Nick to agree to be a secret trustee.

❸ The candidate has confused the law here - stating first that this is a fully secret trust and second that Nick is bound once he receives the instructions from Jordan, regardless of what those instructions might be. The law and application are very confused here: this response demonstrates a misunderstanding of the materials provided and a muddled application of the law to the facts of the case. Notice also that these sentences are quite long and rambling, adding to their lack of clarity. In the assessment, make sure that you use appropriate punctuation and vocabulary to ensure that your answer uses clear and precise language, as required by the assessment criteria.

❹ Again, it seems that the law is wrongly applied, with the candidate misunderstanding the law revealed in the source materials. Although this assessment only lasts an hour, make sure that you take time to read the instructions and sources carefully to avoid making similar mistakes.

❺ The candidate has applied the material law ineffectively. Communication here is not 'in the contents of the envelope' but rather to Nick. The candidate also makes an error by suggesting that communication can be before *death*: as this is a half-secret trust, it needs to happen before or at the time of *executing the codicil*. Applying the correct law is a fundamental skill which cannot be overstated. Here the candidate has incorrectly interpreted the sources supplied, and also seems to have misunderstood the SQE1 FLK on wills.

6 Again the law is wrongly applied from the materials supplied: acceptance is not on 'accepting' the letter, and revocation can be at any reasonable time before Jordan's death. The candidate has not cited the case law provided to support their argument.

7 The conclusion is once again lacking in accuracy and assumes that Nick had no intention to revoke.

Does this answer meet the threshold?

When assessing the second memo against the SQE2 legal research assessment criteria, it is unlikely that it would meet the threshold standard for SQE2 legal research. Although the candidate reaches the same conclusion as in sample answer 1, that Nick must hand over the money, this answer does not demonstrate the candidate's legal research skills sufficiently. The candidate has misinterpreted the law and made assumptions about the facts, which are both poor practices. The answer was also a little brief: it barely mentions the sources and does not show full understanding of how the facts of the case will affect the outcome of any claim by Nick or Sam.

■ KEY POINT CHECKLIST

This chapter has covered the following key knowledge points:

- The SQE2 assessment criteria for legal research, and applying it in the context of wills and the administration of estates regarding both the *commorientes* rule and secret trusts.
- A suggested structure for approaching an SQE2 legal research question.
- Examples of legal research that are likely and unlikely to meet the threshold standard, with full commentary on their strengths and weaknesses.

■ SUMMARY AND REFLECTION

The key to success in the SQE2 legal research assessment is proactive time management once you get into the assessment room so that you use your 60 minutes wisely and efficiently. You will need to use the strategies highlighted in this chapter to help you review the sources so that you identify the ones most relevant to the research question and can quickly and confidently eliminate the irrelevant material. Look for clues in the instructions, and key words that may assist you in selecting what is needed.

Remember that you are being assessed on your ability to produce a research note that is precise and uses acceptable language. Make sure that you clearly apply the materials you have selected to the research issue, and demonstrate how you have found that answer by quoting from the relevant sources.

Before moving on to the next chapter, take some time to reflect and consider what you might still need to work on, and whether you feel completely confident in your legal research skills. Working through this chapter should really make a difference and give you confidence in your research capabilities.

3

Legal writing

■ MAKE SURE YOU KNOW

This chapter covers the skill of legal writing in the context of wills and the administration of estates ('wills'). This is one of the legal skills that may be assessed on day two of the SQE2 assessments (see the Introduction for more detail). Mastering the skill of effective legal writing is also the key to success for all SQE2 written assessments.

The SQE2 legal writing assessment can test your knowledge not only of the processes associated with wills but also of the application of relevant legal principles to those processes. Before attempting the questions in this chapter, boost your knowledge of the subject area by revisiting ***Revise SQE: Wills and the Administration of Estates***, ***Revise SQE: Land Law***, ***Revise SQE: Trusts Law*** and ***Revise SQE: Property Practice***.

This chapter provides examples of how different topics such as partial intestacy, distribution of assets and testamentary clauses such as revocation could arise in the context of an SQE2 legal writing assessment on wills.

■ SQE ASSESSMENT ADVICE

As you work through this chapter, remember to pay particular attention in your revision to:

- selecting relevant information about the legal issue or the client's problem from the material provided in your instructions
- structuring your writing so that your response addresses all parts of the question
- understanding the client's issue from their perspective, focusing only on their legal problem, considerations, priorities, objectives and constraints
- using understandable and simple language to convey facts and information effectively to the client, and correct legal terminology when addressing another legal professional
- identifying the relevant legal principles of the client's case and applying them correctly with sufficient detail in your response
- recognising ethical or professional conduct issues and exercising effective judgement in addressing them, in accordance with the SRA principles and rules of professional conduct.

See the Appendix for the SRA's performance indicators in legal writing and how to demonstrate your competency in this skill.

■ INTRODUCTION TO LEGAL WRITING IN WILLS

Legal writing is a vital skill to develop, not only for the assessment but also for future practice. It will be an essential requirement for you to communicate advice effectively in written form, to avoid negative repercussions for your client or yourself. You should be able to convey information and advice in a way that is persuasive and authoritative, with no ambiguity or confusion. This is especially important when dealing with a client's will because of the sensitive and emotive nature of the matter.

The SQE2 writing assessment in wills is likely to be based on a set of instructions and documents on which you will be asked to produce a written response as the solicitor acting in a matter. Your letter or email might be addressed to a client, a third party, the other side to litigation/client transaction or a partner within a law firm, and it is important to show that you can adopt the appropriate tone and vocabulary for your recipient. This response might be in the context of negotiation and should apply the law clearly and correctly to the client's case. This chapter will provide examples of how you can do this whilst meeting the assessment criteria for SQE2 legal writing in wills.

To create a logical and clear response to your SQE2 assessment, approach the question in a structured manner. Try adopting the following method:

1. Once you have read all the documentation, write down the question(s) being asked of you.
2. Write down the key facts from the instructions that you feel are relevant to answer the question.
3. Check the information in your instructions carefully and then write down the key law/procedure that you think is relevant.
4. Check that the law identified in point 3 above relates back to and answers the question(s) you identified in point 1.
5. Draw up a plan that structures your letter or email around those key facts and legal issues, using headings and subheadings.
6. Complete your written response.
7. Review your answer, keeping in mind the SQE2 legal writing assessment criteria.

Assessment technique

Whilst no one likes to deliver bad news, as per the Code of Conduct for Solicitors, RELs and RFLs remember that you must not mislead or attempt to mislead your clients (rule 1.4). Therefore, you must be comfortable in giving the client information that they might not want to hear and avoid giving false hope that could mislead them. Bear this in mind when approaching the legal writing assessment as you might be asked to address the client directly. You will need to develop strong communication skills to convey advice whilst being sensitive to the client's situation and emotional state of mind.

SQE2 legal writing assessment criteria

Try to remember these points as you construct your response, and refer back to them as you review our sample answers at the end of this chapter:

Skills

1. Include relevant facts.
2. Use a logical structure.
3. Advice/content is client- and recipient-focused.
4. Use clear, precise, concise and acceptable language which is appropriate to the recipient.

Application of law

5. Apply the law correctly to the client's situation.
6. Apply the law comprehensively to the client's situation.
7. Identify any ethical and professional conduct issues and exercise judgement to resolve them honestly and with integrity.

For more detailed support and guidance on how to meet the SQE2 legal writing assessment criteria, see ***Introduction to Written Legal Skills for SQE2***, chapter 3, Legal writing.

In chapter 6 of ***Revise SQE: Wills and the Administration of Estates***, we considered the rules relating to property falling outside an estate. Question 1 below demonstrates how your knowledge of this topic could be tested in the context and format of an SQE2 legal writing assessment.

QUESTION 1

Email to candidate

From: Partner
Sent: 13 September 202#
To: Candidate
Subject: Walter Singler (Deceased)

We have been instructed by Billy Singler (aged 68), the brother of Walter Singler. Walter died on 24 July 202# at the age of 72, leaving a will (see Attachment 1). Billy is in a very emotional and confused state of mind; he is concerned that the will is now invalid because some members of Walter's family mentioned as beneficiaries in the will have predeceased him. Walter's family tree is included as Attachment 2.

Walter was not married and had no children. Walter and Billy were living together at the time of Walter's death. They jointly owned a property and its contents in Oxford. Their parents, Raffiel and Mabel, predeceased Walter. Walter and Billy's sister, Bonnie Baker, died some time ago and is survived by three of her four children, the nephews and nieces mentioned by Walter in the attached will. Walter was an avid collector of Roman artefacts and also owned a considerable amount of shares.

Specifically, Walter held the following assets in his sole name unless otherwise stated:

1. House in Oxford (value £350,000) owned jointly by Walter and his brother Billy as beneficial joint tenants. No outstanding mortgage.
2. Collection of Roman coins and a Roman helmet (value £3,000).
3. Remaining contents of the house (value £5,000) held by Walter and Billy as beneficial joint tenants.
4. Items of clothing, a watch and some artwork (value £800).
5. HSBC current account (balance £3,750).
6. NatWest deposit account (balance £18,400).
7. Quoted stocks and shares with no controlling interest (value £640,000).
8. Range Rover car (value £15,000).

Walter had no debts. We intend to advise Billy at a later date on inheritance tax, and also how funeral expenses affect the estate. Billy has also told us that he wishes to remain in the property he owned with Walter, but there is no need at this point to advise on this in any detail.

Please write an email addressed to me so that I can pass some information to our client Billy Singler, addressing the following questions:

1. **Which assets pass outside Walter's succession estate, and how will those assets be distributed?**

2. **Which assets comprise Walter's succession estate, and what is their value?**
3. **Explain how Walter's succession estate will be distributed: identify each beneficiary and describe what proportion of the estate they will inherit. There is no need to give values in monetary terms.**

Please do not include any other information at this point.

Thanks

Partner

Attachments:

1. Walter Singler's will
2. Singler family tree

Attachment 1

THIS IS THE LAST WILL AND TESTAMENT of me WALTER SINGLER of Mansion House, Oxford, Oxfordshire - retired

1. I REVOKE all former wills and testamentary dispositions made by me
2. I APPOINT my friend FINN CRONIN and my brother BILLY SINGLER (hereinafter called 'my Executors') to be the executors of my will
3. I GIVE the following specific legacies free of tax and costs of transfer
   a) my Roman helmet to my nephew Jake Baker
   b) all of my artwork to my niece Jinny Baker
   c) my watch to my niece Joan Baker
   d) my Roman coins to my nephew Danny Baker
   e) all my personal chattels as defined in section 55(1)(x) of the Administration of Estates Act 1925 not otherwise specifically bequeathed by this my will or any codicil hereto together with any of the specific legacies in clauses 3 a) to 3 d) which shall fail for any reason to my brother Billy Singler
4. I GIVE the following pecuniary legacies free of tax
   a) the sum of five thousand pounds (£5,000) to my sister Bonnie Baker
   b) the sum of one thousand pounds (£1,000) to each of my said nephews and nieces, Jake, Jinny, Joan and Danny
5. I GIVE all the rest and residue of my estate both real and personal whatsoever and wheresoever SUBJECT TO the payment of my debts funeral and testamentary expenses and legacies unto my mother Mabel Singler absolutely
6. MY EXECUTORS shall have the following powers in addition to their powers under the general law
   a) In any case where they have an obligation or a discretion under the provisions of my will or under the general law to pay income or capital to or for the benefit of a minor to discharge that obligation or to exercise that discretion if they think fit by making payment either to a parent or guardian of the minor or to the minor personally if of the age of sixteen at least and so that their respective receipts shall be a full discharge to my Executors who shall not be required to see to the application of any income or capital
   b) To exercise the power of appropriation conferred by section 41 of the Administration of Estates Act 1925 without obtaining any of the consents required by that section and even though one or more of them may be beneficially interested

IN WITNESS whereof I have hereunto set my hand this 6 January 1998

Signed by the above named WALTER SINGLER *Walter Singler*

In our joint presence and then by us in his

Ronnie Wilkinson *Jason Tripp*

Ronnie Wilkinson
(Chauffeur)
Main Cottage,
Oxford

Jason Tripp
Accountant
Beconsfield House,
Beconsfield

Attachment 2

Singler family tree

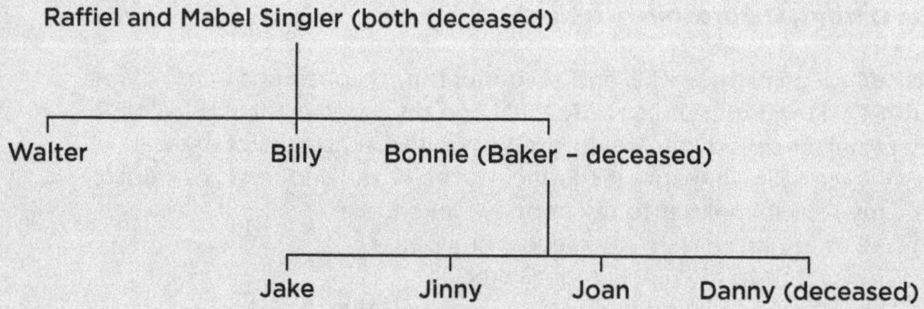

* * *

■ YOUR TURN

Have a go at answering question 1, remembering the guidance on pages 64–66.

- Remember the structured approach in the SRA's assessment criteria on page 65.
- Create a list of the most salient legal issues raised by the question, especially the assets and whether they form part of Walter's estate.
- Timings are important: you will need to prepare and write your answer in 30 minutes.

SQE1 Functioning legal knowledge link
Remember from chapter 6 of ***Revise SQE: Wills and Administration of Estates*** that the rules of property passing outside an estate must be applied when a deceased leaves assets in an estate with or without a will. As there is a will here, but also perhaps partial intestacy, distribution of assets passing inside and outside the estate will need to be analysed carefully. Property held as joint tenants before death passes to a surviving joint tenant through survivorship.

EVALUATING YOUR ANSWER

When you have attempted question 1, mark it yourself against the SQE2 legal writing assessment criteria. Do you think your attempt met the threshold standard?

Now compare your attempt with the following key legal points and two sample answers to question 1. A circled number indicates that commentary is provided for this part of the answer. The commentary explains whether or not the sample satisfies the assessment criteria, and accordingly whether it is likely to meet the SQE2 threshold standard.

➥Key legal points: question 1

You will need to focus on the following points in order to answer the question:

Property owned by the deceased as a beneficial joint tenant

- The key principle of a joint tenancy is that, when one joint tenant dies, their interest in the property automatically passes on to the surviving joint tenant(s) because of the principle of survivorship. When the deceased joint tenant dies, their interest in the property is 'extinguished' and passes on automatically to the survivors.
- The house in Oxford and its contents were owned jointly by Walter and Billy. The interest under a joint tenancy therefore never becomes part of the deceased's estate, because it is extinguished at the very moment of death.
- A will containing a provision that someone is to inherit an interest under a joint tenancy will be of no effect.
- Half the value of the joint tenancy interest may still be subject to inheritance tax.

Partial intestacy

- Full intestacy involves a situation where a will does not exist or has totally failed. This is not the case here but a partial intestacy is a situation in which a will exists but some of the legacies fail because some problem has arisen with a specific gift in the will.
- There are a number of reasons why a testamentary gift can fail (see chapter 3 of ***Revise SQE Wills and Administration of Estates***). For example: it was made to someone who witnessed the will; the beneficiary predeceased the testator and the gift has lapsed; or even the beneficiary does not want the gift and has disclaimed it.
- Usually, if there is a residuary clause in the will, all of the failed gifts mentioned above would simply fall into residue. That is one reason why a well-drafted will always contain a residuary clause.
- However, if the will does not contain a residuary clause, or if the residuary clause is itself defective - as in this case, where the residuary beneficiary has predeceased the testator - then there is nowhere for the failed gift to go. Other parts of the will may be perfectly valid and properly executed, but this particular gift cannot be made.
- In these circumstances, there is a partial intestacy and the personal representatives must, pursuant to s 49(1) Administration of Estates Act 1925, apply the intestacy rules to that gift.

Where the partial intestacy rules apply

- Where the deceased leaves neither spouse or issue, as with Walter, the personal representatives move through the 'statutory list' until they find a relative of the partially intestate deceased who fits the bill, and then stop.
- If they are directed to apply the statutory trusts, then they must do so. It should be noted that the 'first' on the list here would be Walter's full brothers and sisters on the statutory trusts. If any sibling has already predeceased Walter, then their issue come next.

■ SAMPLE ANSWER 1 TO QUESTION 1

From: Candidate
Sent: 13 September 202#
To: Partner
Subject: Walter Singler (Deceased)

You have asked me to respond in relation to the matter of Walter Singler (deceased) following concerns raised by his brother Billy. What follows is my advice on this matter and specifically the questions you raised. ❶

1. Which assets pass outside Walter's succession estate, and how will those assets be distributed? ❷

The items excluded from the estate are those that are held as joint tenants. This means that the rules of survivorship apply. The house in Oxford (item 1) and its contents (item 3) automatically pass to Billy without becoming part of Walter's estate. ❸

2. Which assets comprise Walter's succession estate, and what is their value?

All remaining items (item 2 and items 4–8) are included in the succession estate and will pass under Walter's will. There are issues with some of the legacies as it appears that some of the beneficiaries/legatees (Bonnie and Danny) have predeceased Walter, although that does not mean they do not fall under his estate.

As such, the total value of the succession estate is **£680,950**. ❹

3. Explain how Walter's succession estate will be distributed: identify each beneficiary and describe what they will inherit

The fact that some legatees have predeceased Walter will affect how his assets will be distributed and to whom. The key clauses in the will that are at issue are clauses 3, 4 and 5, and I will take each in turn.

Clause 3

- Clause 3 (a): the Roman helmet passes to Jake, who is still alive.
- Clause 3 (b): all of the artwork passes to Jinny, who is still alive.
- Clause 3 (c): the watch passes to Joan, who is still alive.
- Clause 3 (d): the Roman coins should have passed to Danny but, as Danny predeceased Walter, this gift fails.
- Clause 3 (e): all assets that qualify as 'chattels' that have not yet been distributed pass to Billy. This includes the Roman coins and the items not already mentioned in the will – Walter's clothing and his Range Rover. Note that chattels do not include money or money interests, only items that were used and enjoyed by the deceased on a regular basis. ❺

Clause 4

- Clause 4 (a): the pecuniary legacy of £5,000 to Bonnie fails and is not paid as she has predeceased Walter.
- Clause 4 (b): pecuniary legacies of £1,000 will be paid to Jake, Jinny and Joan. The legacy to Danny fails and is not paid as he predeceased Walter.
- The value of these failed gifts (£6,000) is added to the estate residue. ❻

Clause 5

The residue of Walter's succession estate should pass to his mother, Mabel. However, she predeceased Walter so this gift fails. Walter's will does not dispose fully of his assets so he died partially intestate. This means that, for this failed gift, the statutory rules apply in terms of distribution in the absence of any substitution clause in favour of an alternative beneficiary. ❼

Walter died leaving no spouse, children or surviving parent, so his siblings of the whole blood inherit the entire residuary estate on the statutory trusts. Billy takes his half share of the residue outright. As Bonnie has predeceased Walter, her surviving children will inherit by substitution the other half of the residue that she would have taken had she survived; Bonnie's half will be divided into thirds, with Jake, Jinny and Joan taking a share each. Billy, Jake, Jinny and Joan can benefit under intestacy in addition to any other inheritance they are entitled to under Walter's will. ❽

COMMENTARY

❶ This is an excellent start. It is always good practice to have an 'opening gambit' that sets the tone and context of the written response and identifies the task that has been requested. This demonstrates the skill of writing a client-focused letter.

❷ The candidate effectively uses the questions of this task as numbered headings for each section of the answer. This is an extremely useful structure and gives great clarity for the recipient. The SQE2 assessor will also clearly see that all aspects of the question have been addressed and a logical structure has been adopted, as required by the assessment criteria.

❸ The candidate succinctly explains how assets are normally distributed under a will, outlining the effects of joint tenancy and survivorship on the estate. The candidate brings clarity to the response by referring not only to the specific items (the house and its contents) but also using the names of the client and his brother, Billy and Walter, to avoid any confusion or ambiguity.

❹ The candidate presents another clear and concise answer to the partner's questions, satisfying many elements of the assessment criteria. They have correctly calculated the total value of the remaining items mentioned in the will and demonstrated a client-focused approach by swiftly applying their knowledge of legal principles to the issue of some beneficiaries and legatees to Walter's estate having predeceased him.

❺ The candidate has impressively set out the assets at clause 3 in the will and clarified how these assets will be distributed and why. The candidate uses clear language that would be easily understood by the client to explain why the car and the clothing are categorised as chattels but the pecuniary legacies are not.

❻ The candidate has also effectively dealt with clause 4 and the failed gifts. Rather than just list them, the candidate has clearly explained why the gifts have failed and the effect of those failures, that is, they accumulate to the residue.

❼ The candidate demonstrates their ability to apply the law correctly and comprehensively to the client's situation here, by stating that there is partial intestacy because the residuary estate should vest in Walter's mother Mabel, but that Mabel has predeceased Walter with no changes to the will. The candidate goes on to explain the effect of partial intestacy, using appropriate legal terminology for the partner to whom the email is addressed. Many aspects of the assessment criteria are being met here.

❽ Finally, the candidate concludes with a thorough but effective explanation of this partial intestacy and highlights the statutory distribution order, correctly identifying that the residue will vest in Billy and in Bonnie's remaining children. The concluding remark that property can be left as a legacy in a will and also through partial intestacy to the same beneficiaries/legatees is excellent.

Does this answer meet the threshold?

The sample answer contains all of the information relating to the distribution of assets that the client requires and that the candidate has been asked to provide. It discusses and applies the relevant principles and statutory rules and how they apply to the scenario, showing a strong client-focused approach. It is clear, succinct and legally correct: the candidate has effectively identified which items pass under the will, those that pass outside the will and those that pass under partial intestacy. It is therefore likely to meet the threshold standard for SQE2 legal writing.

Now consider the second sample answer to question 1.

■ SAMPLE ANSWER 2 TO QUESTION 1

From: Candidate
Sent: 13 September 202#
To: Partner
Subject: Billy Singler ❶

Assets to be distributed? ❷

Generally assets in a will form part of the deceased's estate, unless the will itself is invalid. The will here is valid but there are problems. Some of these items need to be excluded from the estate, such as the House in Oxford as that is a joint tenancy. This means that the rules of survivorship apply where these items automatically pass to the surviving joint tenant without those items becoming part of the deceased's estate. That means that the house in Oxford (item 1) automatically passes to Billy without them becoming part of Walter's estate. ❸

Assets under the estate

All remaining items are included in the succession estate and will pass under Walter's will.

The items under the estate are as follows:

Collection of Roman coins and a Roman helmet (value £3,000).
Remaining contents of the house (value £5,000).
Items of clothing, a watch and some artwork (value £800).
HSBC current account (balance £3,750).
NatWest deposit account (balance £18,400).
Quoted stocks and shares with no controlling interest (value £640,000).
Range Rover car (value £15,000).

As such the total value of the succession estate is **£685,950**. ❹

Who gets what? ❺

Clause 3

- Clause 3 (a): the Roman helmet passes to Jake – Jake is still alive.
- Clause 3 (b): all of the artwork passes to Jinny – Jinny is still alive.
- Clause 3 (c): the watch passes to Joan – Joan is still alive.
- Clause 3 (d): the Roman coins should have passed to Danny, but this gift fails because Danny predeceased Walter.
- Clause 3 (e): All assets that qualify as 'chattels' that have not yet been distributed pass to Billy. This includes the Roman coins. ❻

Clause 4

- Clause 4 (a): the pecuniary legacy of £5,000 to Bonnie fails and is not paid as she has predeceased Walter.
- Clause 4 (b): Pecuniary legacies of £1,000 will be paid to Jake, Jinny and Joan. Danny predeceased Walter but his legacy of £1,000 will be shared between Jake, Jinny and Joan. ❼

Clause 5
The residuary estate is everything that has not been given away by an earlier part of the will.

By virtue of clause 5, the residue of Walter's succession estate should pass to his mother Mabel. However, she predeceased Walter so this gift fails. Walter's will does not dispose fully of his assets so he has died intestate. This means that for this failed gift, the statutory rules apply in terms of distribution. ❽

Intestacy rules

Walter died leaving no spouse or children, so his father will take the entire residue under the rules of intestacy. If his father dies within 28 days of Walter, then Walter's siblings of the whole blood inherit the entire residuary estate on the statutory trusts. Walter had two siblings, Billy and Bonnie. Billy takes his half share of the residue outright. As Bonnie has predeceased Walter, her surviving children will inherit by substitution the other half of the residue that she would have taken had she survived; her half will be divided into thirds, with Jake, Jinny and Joan taking a share each (this is by operation of the statutory trust). ❾

COMMENTARY

❶ This is not a great start. The subject matter does not mirror the email from the partner and does not identify the deceased by name (Walter).

❷ It is good practice to have an opening paragraph that sets the tone and context of the written response and identifies the task that has been requested. This is missing here. This answer also suffers from a poor structure, as the candidate has chosen not to use the questions posed as headings for each section of the answer. This leads to a lack of clarity: the answer is not easy to follow as the candidate has not mirrored the numbering used in the question.

❸ The candidate has tried to explain how assets are normally distributed under a will, and does identify the issue of items passing under and outside the will, but this response lacks detail. The opening is vague, and though there is reference to joint tenancy and survivorship this is not explained. More importantly, the candidate seems to have missed the fact the house contents are also held as joint tenants. This will cause problems later on. Note also that the writing in this paragraph appears rushed and is somewhat clunky and repetitive. You need to develop good time-keeping skills for this assessment, which includes setting aside some time at the end of the assessment to review your answer and polish the language where necessary.

❹ It can be good practice to set out the key facts as given in instructions so the client can quickly see the relevant assets and how they may be included or ignored for the purposes of distribution. The candidate has not quite managed to achieve this, however: there is again a lack of detail, and not all items that fall under the estate are listed, as the question requires. The items and their values are inaccurate as the contents have been included, which would also pass under survivorship (this creates an error of £5,000 in the calculations). It would have been clearer if the candidate had numbered the items, to avoid any ambiguity. The candidate has also failed to mention the impact of some beneficiaries/legatees predeceasing Walter, which indicates a lack of focus on the details of the client's circumstances.

❺ The candidate has used rather informal language as the subheading, and again is not following the question layout. They are missing the opportunity to show the assessor that they can form a written response with a logical structure, as required by the assessment criteria.

❻ Although the candidate has set down the assets at clause 3 in the will and clearly explains how these assets will be distributed and why, the explanation of 'chattels' is brief and lacks substance. There is no clarification for the client of why the car and the clothing are categorised as chattels but the pecuniary legacies are not.

7 The candidate has identified the legacy correctly in clause 4 (a) but makes an error in clause 4 (b): Danny's portion would accumulate to the residue rather than being shared amongst his surviving siblings. This mistake affects the accuracy of the calculations further. The candidate also neglects to explain the effect of the failed gifts on the residue. The client requires more clarity and accuracy.

8 The candidate deals with clause 5 and realises that the residuary estate should vest in Walter's mother, Mabel, but that the will has not changed since Mabel's death. However, the candidate uses the term 'intestate' rather than 'partially intestate' - and this is an important distinction. The candidate fails to clearly explain the effect of partial intestacy and does not refer to a possible substitution clause in the alternative. The law is not being correctly applied to the client's circumstances here.

9 The candidate makes a major error in missing the fact from the materials (the family tree in Attachment 2) that Walter's father, Raffiel, has also predeceased Walter, so the conclusion that Raffiel takes half the residue is incorrect. It is also incorrect to point to a 28-day timeframe as this only applies to a spouse, not other family members, surviving the deceased. This response therefore shows a lack of attention to detail and also gaps in the candidate's legal knowledge. The candidate does correctly identify that the residue will vest in Billy and Bonnie's remaining children, but this does not compensate for the impact of the other errors on the candidate's response.

Does this answer meet the threshold?

When assessing the second written response against the SQE2 legal writing assessment criteria, it is unlikely that it would meet the threshold standard. The candidate has misinterpreted or misapplied the law and made errors in relation to the distribution of assets (the jointly owned contents) and the fact that Raffiel has predeceased Walter. The answer was also a little brief and does not show a full understanding of how assets are distributed in this scenario. It is vital to read through all materials carefully: the family tree was ignored here, with serious consequences for the client's advice.

SQE2 can assess any of the areas on the SQE1 wills specification. Below is another example of how a different part of the specification could arise in the context of SQE2 legal writing in wills. This time it is based on formalities and revocation.

■ QUESTION 2

Email to candidate

From: Julius Gold (Partner)
Sent: 13 August 202#
To: Candidate
Subject: Margaret Smart (Deceased)

We have been approached by Clara Simmons, of 41 River Road, Nottingham NG42 4ED, in relation to the will of her aunt, Margaret Smart. The background facts below are taken from the recent interview with Clara.

It seems that Margaret, a retired art teacher, executed a valid will in 2018 (**Attachment 1**) and left her entire estate to her niece, Clara. In 2021, after an argument with Clara, Margaret wrote a new will on a piece of paper (**Attachment 2**). This left her estate to her neighbour, Tom Matthews, who had been helping her with daily errands. Margaret signed the document but did not have any witnesses present.

In 2023, Margaret reconciled with Clara and told several friends that she intended to 'tear up that silly note and go back to the original plan'. She never physically destroyed the 2021 document but she misplaced it and never mentioned it again. Upon Margaret's death last month, both documents were found in her desk drawer: the 2018 will neatly filed, and the 2021 handwritten note folded and unsigned on the back.

Tom claims the 2021 note was Margaret's final will and should be upheld. Clara argues that the 2018 will remains valid and that the 2021 note was not properly executed and did not revoke the 2018 will.

Please write a letter addressed to Clara to be signed by me, advising whether the 2018 will has been revoked and which document is likely to be upheld as Margaret's valid will.

Thanks

Julius

Attachments:

1. Margaret Smart's will
2. Margaret Smart's handwritten note

Attachment 1

Last Will and Testament of Margaret Smart

I, Margaret Smart, of 100 Burton Drive, Nottingham NG44 2BY, being of sound mind and disposing memory, do hereby declare this to be my Last Will and Testament, hereby revoking all prior wills and codicils made by me

1. I appoint Clara Simmons, my niece, as the sole executor of this will
2. I give, devise, and bequeath all my real and personal property, including any residuary estate, to my niece, Clara Simmons, absolutely
3. If Clara Simmons predeceases me, I give my Residuary Estate to my neighbour Tom Matthews, for his own use and benefit absolutely

IN WITNESS WHEREOF, I have hereunto set my hand this 1st day of July, 2018
Margaret Smart

Witnessed by:
John Smithers

1. Signed: John Smithers

Name: Address: John Smithers, 2 Manor Farm, Forestgrove, Nottingham NG37 3EL
Pauline Foulds

2. Signed: Pauline Foulds

Name: Address: Pauline Foulds, 11 Burton Drive, Nottingham, NG44 2BR

Attachment 2

I, Margaret Smart, wish to change my will. I no longer want Clara to inherit my estate.

Instead, I leave everything I own to my neighbour, Tom Matthews, who has been kind and helpful to me.

This is my new will.

Signed: Margaret Smart

Date: 14th October 2021

■ YOUR TURN

Have a go at answering question 2, remembering the guidance on pages 64–66.

- Remember the structured approach in the SRA's assessment criteria earlier in the chapter.
- Create a list of the most salient legal issues raised by the question, especially the validity of the handwritten note in 2021.
- Timings are important: you will need to prepare and write your answer in 30 minutes.

SQE1 Functioning legal knowledge link
Remember from ***Revise SQE: Wills and Administration of Estates***, chapter 4, that necessary formalities must be followed for a will to be valid, and if revocation, whole or partial is to be effective, the necessary formalities must again be followed. The key issue here is whether the handwritten note successfully revokes the original 2018 will and as such whether Tom will benefit rather than Clara.

EVALUATING YOUR ANSWER

When you have attempted question 2, mark it yourself against the SQE2 legal writing assessment criteria. Do you think your attempt met the threshold standard?

Now compare your attempt with the following key legal points and two sample answers to question 2. A circled number indicates that commentary is provided for this part of the answer. The commentary explains whether or not the sample satisfies the assessment criteria, and accordingly whether it is likely to meet the SQE2 threshold standard.

➥Key legal points: question 2

Formalities under s 9 Wills Act 1837

- A will must be in writing, signed by the testator and witnessed by two independent witnesses.
- The 2021 note, though signed, lacked witnesses and therefore does not satisfy statutory requirements. It is invalid as a will.

Revocation of a will

- Revocation occurs by marriage, execution of a later valid will or physical destruction with intent.
- The 2021 document was not validly executed, so it cannot revoke the 2018 will.

- Margaret did not destroy the 2018 will. There is evidence of an intention to return to it.
- The 2021 note was not destroyed but misplaced; however, since it was never valid, it has no revocatory effect.

Statements of intention

- Margaret's comments in 2023 reinforce that she did not intend the 2021 note to operate as her final testamentary disposition.

■ SAMPLE ANSWER 1 TO QUESTION 2

[*The law firm's address and contact details*]

Private & Confidential
Ms Clara Simmons
41 River Road
Nottingham
NG42 4ED
13 August 202#

Dear Ms Simmons, ❶

Re: Estate of Margaret Smart (Deceased)

We write further to your instructions regarding the estate of your late aunt, Margaret, who sadly passed away last month. We appreciate that this is a difficult time for you, but we hope that what follows will clarify the position. ❷

Background to the matter

In 2018, Margaret executed a valid will leaving her entire estate to you. In 2021, following a disagreement, she prepared a handwritten note purporting to leave her estate to her neighbour, Tom. This document was signed by Margaret but not witnessed. In 2023, after reconciling with you, Margaret told several friends she intended to disregard the 2021 note and return to her original plan. She did not destroy the 2021 note but subsequently misplaced it and did not mention it again. Upon her death in 202#, both the 2018 will and the 2021 handwritten note were found in her desk. ❸

Tom Matthews now claims that the 2021 note represents Margaret's final will, whilst you maintain that the 2018 will remains valid. It is necessary, therefore, to advise you as to whether the 2021 note is, in effect, a revocation of the 2018 will. The facts as set out above will help you to understand the legal position. Revocation of a will is a serious matter with potentially serious consequences; the law requires certain formalities to be complied with and a clear intention on the part of Margaret.

Legal position

1. Execution requirements – a will must be signed by the testator in the presence of two witnesses, who must also sign in the presence of the testator. The 2021 note was not witnessed and therefore does not satisfy the statutory requirements. It is invalid and cannot take effect as a will.
2. Revocation of earlier wills – a will is revoked by marriage, by a subsequent valid will or by destruction with intent to revoke. Since the 2021 document was not a valid will, it did not revoke the 2018 will.

3. Margaret's intention – Margaret's statements in 2023 reinforce the conclusion that she did not intend the 2021 note to stand. Her subsequent conduct of misplacing the note and failing to mention it also supports the position that she reverted to her 2018 will. ❹

Conclusion

The 2018 will remains valid and is the document the court is most likely to uphold. Tom's claim is unlikely to succeed, as the 2021 note is not a properly executed will and did not revoke the 2018 will. ❺

Next steps

You should proceed to apply for a grant of probate on the basis of the 2018 will. Should Tom seek to contest the matter, we will be able to defend your position relying on the invalidity of the 2021 note and Margaret's clear intention to uphold her original will. Do contact us if you discover any further evidence in the form of other documents in your possession.

Please let us know if you wish us to prepare the probate application on your behalf or respond formally to any claim made by Tom.

Yours sincerely,

Julius Gold (Partner) ❻

COMMENTARY

❶ The candidate has used the correct title and terminology here, addressing the letter to the client and using their surname. This is the correct format for a letter to a client, although it is acceptable to use the first name for an existing client with an ongoing relationship with the firm. This does not seem to be the case here. The address is also accurately reproduced.

❷ This is good practice: empathy is demonstrated without being overly emotive. Bereaved clients are likely to be emotional and therefore require clarity and an objective, non-emotive response from their solicitor.

❸ There is good background here, with the relevant facts of the case repeated to the client to provide absolute clarity; this meets the assessment criteria of including the correct information and being client-focused. Furthermore, not only does the candidate effectively explain the validity of the 2018 will; they also explain the invalidity of the 2021 note and the effect of Margaret's seeming intention in 2023, which may provide further evidence as to the invalidity of the 2021 note.

❹ The candidate has used the material effectively, applying the correct law without citing it as this is a letter to a client. The key legal issues are addressed and accurate; precise advice is given so that the client can understand the position.

❺ As above, the candidate demonstrates excellent application of the legal position to draw an appropriate and accurate conclusion. Clara would not be in any doubt as to the strength of her assertions here that the 2021 note is neither a will nor an adequate revocation of the 2018 will. The detail here is correct and impressively presented with great clarity, exactly as the question requires and therefore meeting the assessment criteria.

❻ Finally, the candidate ends the advice clearly and succinctly, including clear next steps and an accurate and appropriate sign-off. Where the client is an individual who has met the sender of the letter, the closing sign off should be, as here, 'Yours sincerely'. The name of the partner is also included, as requested in the instructions.

Does this answer meet the threshold?

The sample answer contains all of the information and application of the law relating to revocation of a will and the formalities needed to create and revoke a will. It produces a letter exactly as the client requires and that the candidate has been asked to provide. The letter discusses the relevant formalities and correct legal position, and how these apply to the scenario. The answer is client-focused and relevant at all times. The language and style of writing is clear, succinct and appropriate for the recipient. This response is therefore likely to meet the threshold standard for SQE2 legal writing.

Now consider the second sample answer to question 2.

SAMPLE ANSWER 2 TO QUESTION 2

13 August 202#
Private & Confidential

Dear Clara Simmons ❶

Re: Estate of Margaret Smart (Deceased)

We write further to your instructions regarding the estate of your deceased aunt, Margaret, who tragically passed away last month. ❷

Background facts

In 2018, Margaret executed a valid will leaving her entire estate to you. In 2021, following a falling out with you, she prepared a handwritten note trying to leave her estate to her neighbour, Tom. This document was signed by Margaret but not witnessed. I am sure you know this is incorrect. In 2023, after making up with you, Margaret told people she intended to ignore the 2021 note and leave it all to you. ☺ She did not destroy the 2021 note but lost it and never mentioned it again. When she tragically died last month, both the 2018 will and the 2021 handwritten note were found in her desk.

It seems that Tom now claims that the 2021 note represents Margaret's final will, whilst you say that the 2018 will remains valid. Of course – you're right!!! ❸

Legals ❹

- The law says that under the Wills Act 1837, a will must be signed by the deceased. The 2021 note was signed by Margaret, and on that point it therefore does satisfy the statutory requirements. It is valid, and so it is like a will.
- Revocation: a will is revoked by a subsequent valid will, by destruction with intent to revoke or by getting married. Although the 2021 document was a valid will, it did not revoke the 2018 will as the 2018 will was not destroyed.
- Margaret's conduct: Margaret's statements in 2023 seem to suggest that she did not intend the 2021 note to be her new will, but this is not relevant at all as the original will was never destroyed. ❺

Conclusion

The 2018 will remains valid because it was never destroyed. Tom's claim WILL FAIL, as the 2021 note did not revoke the 2018 will. ❻

Next steps

- You should move FAST to apply for probate using the 2018 will.
- Should Tom argue, we will fight back! We can say that the 2021 note is totally useless for him.

If you would like us to write to Tom and tell him to drop any thoughts of bringing a claim we would be more than happy to do that.

Yours sincerely,

Trainee Solicitor ❼

COMMENTARY

❶ The candidate has used the incorrect title and terminology here, addressing the letter to the client using their first name and surname. This is the incorrect format for a letter to a client, and the candidate has also omitted to include the client's address. This indicates a careless approach to the professional standards required of a legal letter, and would create a poor first impression on the SQE2 assessor.

❷ This is poor practice: the candidate is correct to demonstrate empathy with the client, but using the word 'tragically' is excessively emotive. This is not appropriate language, as required by the assessment criteria.

❸ There is an attempt at providing background to the matter here for the client, but there are a number of omissions as to detail. The candidate does not effectively explain the validity of the 2018 will, nor do they properly explain the invalidity of the 2021 note and the effect of Margaret's seeming intention in 2023, which may provide further evidence as to the invalidity of the 2021 note. The tone in this paragraph is also too informal and familiar. Telling the client that 'I am sure you know' and 'Of course – you're right' is not the correct approach and does not adhere to professional conduct. Emojis and multiple exclamation marks are also highly inappropriate for a professional letter and should never be included.

❹ The heading 'Legals' is inappropriate and unhelpful in a client letter. Make sure that you structure your letter logically and include clear, informative headings to assist the client in following your advice. Also, although you need to convey the information clearly, beware of overusing the bullet list format as this candidate has done in this answer.

❺ The candidate makes a fatal legal error in this section by suggesting that because Margaret signed the 2021 note it is akin to a valid will. As such the candidate has not used the materials effectively and instead both applies the law incorrectly and contradicts statements given earlier in the answer. The key legal issues are not addressed with accuracy, and precise advice is therefore not given. The client is likely to be more confused than reassured about her position after reading this letter, and the candidate fails to meet the assessment criteria here.

❻ Although the overall conclusion is correct, the legal reasoning is wrong and a key point is missed. The lack of destruction of the 2018 will is only part of the reason for the non-revocation; more importantly, the 2021 note was not signed by two witnesses so it was never a valid will. Clara is likely to be in some doubt as to the strength of her assertions that the 2021 note is neither a will nor an adequate revocation of the 2018 will, as the detail here is incorrect and lacks clarity. A further point about appropriate language: using upper-case letters for emphasis ('WILL FAIL') is not professional or acceptable when writing to a client.

❼ Finally, the candidate ends the advice in a sloppy, casual fashion, stating that they will 'fight back' and practically offering to threaten Tom into dropping any claim to the estate. This is a clear breach of professional conduct, and the advice to 'move FAST' is unhelpful and inappropriately expressed. The candidate also signs the letter using their own name, which is not what the instructions stated.

Does this answer meet the threshold?

When assessing the second letter against the SQE2 legal writing assessment criteria, it is unlikely that it would meet the threshold standard. The candidate has misinterpreted the law and made errors, particularly in relation to the validity and formalities required for the 2021 note. The answer was also a little brief, badly structured and poorly presented: it includes informal and emotive language, emojis, letters in upper case and frequent exclamation marks. The letter fails to show full understanding of how the facts of the case will affect the outcome of any claim by Tom.

■ KEY POINT CHECKLIST

This chapter has covered the following key knowledge points:

- The SQE2 assessment criteria for legal writing and how to apply them in the context of wills and the administration of estates.
- A suggested structure for approaching an SQE2 case and legal writing question.
- Examples of legal writing that are likely and unlikely to meet the threshold standard, with full commentary on their strengths and weaknesses.

■ SUMMARY AND REFLECTION

When beginning the SQE2 legal writing assessment, make sure that you read the question carefully. Think about the legal points the question is asking of you and draw up a brief plan to follow so that your answer will be logically and clearly structured. This assessment only lasts 30 minutes, so you need to think quickly and decisively.

The assessor will be judging your ability to apply the law both correctly and comprehensively. As well as pinpointing the relevant law, you will need to explain how it can be applied to the wider context of the client's scenario and the more specific points. Practise writing letters to the appropriate audience, including the correct legal terminology when addressing another legal professional, or avoiding legal jargon and explaining matters in clear, simple English when addressing a client.

Now take time to reflect and consider what you might still need to work on, and whether you feel completely confident in your legal writing skills in the context of wills and the administration of estates.

4

Legal drafting

■ MAKE SURE YOU KNOW

This chapter covers the skill of legal drafting in the context of wills and the administration of estates ('wills'). This is one of the legal skills that may be assessed on day two of the SQE2 assessments (see the Introduction for more detail). Drafting is obviously an essential part of working in the area of wills, and you will need to develop a strong set of legal drafting skills to succeed as a practising solicitor.

In the SQE2 assessment you will be required to analyse the key facts of a given scenario and draft appropriately to reflect the client's situation. Your knowledge of the processes associated with wills will be tested, and also your ability to apply the relevant legal principles to those processes. Before attempting the questions in this chapter, refresh your functioning legal knowledge of this subject area by revisiting ***Revise SQE: Wills and the Administration of Estates***, ***Revise SQE: Land Law***, ***Revise SQE: Trusts Law*** and ***Revise SQE: Property Practice***.

This chapter provides examples of how different topics such as amending testamentary clauses and completing affidavits when applying for probate could arise in the context of an SQE2 legal drafting assessment on wills.

■ SQE ASSESSMENT ADVICE

As you work through this chapter and the exercises, remember to pay particular attention in your revision to:

- using understandable and simple language to convey facts and information effectively
- using correct legal terminology, and paying close attention to dates, names, addresses and even postcodes when drafting legal forms or templates
- selecting relevant information about the client's problem from the material provided in your instructions, which could contain complex legal and financial detail in relation to assets
- applying your legal knowledge to substantiate your drafting so that you produce a legally correct document
- understanding and addressing the client's problem from their perspective, to produce a comprehensive document that is legally watertight and deals with the client's financial considerations, priorities, objectives and constraints
- where relevant, recognising ethical and professional conduct issues and exercising effective judgement in addressing them, in accordance with the SRA principles and rules of professional conduct.

See the Appendix for the SRA's performance indicators in legal drafting and how to demonstrate your competency in this skill.

■ INTRODUCTION TO LEGAL DRAFTING IN WILLS

Legal drafting is a vital skill for legal practice. As a solicitor, and depending on your area of practice, you may be required to draft a wide variety of legal documents. In the area of wills, this could include the following:

- deeds of trust
- alterations and amendments to wills
- estate planning.

Drafting these documents requires a thorough understanding of legal principles, close attention to detail and the ability to tailor documents to the specific needs of clients. You will need to show your SQE2 assessor that you have developed strong skills in these areas and are competent to practise.

In the SQE2 assessment, you will be provided with a memorandum in the form of an email from a partner that explains the legal drafting that is required. You might be asked to draft from a precedent or amend a document already drafted. You may also be required to draft a document without the benefit of any precedent or existing document. This chapter will provide examples of how you can do this and meet the SQE2 assessment criteria.

We recommend that you approach your SQE2 legal drafting assessment in a structured manner. Try adopting the following method:

1. Once you have read all the documentation, write down the question(s) being asked of you. It is vital to know exactly what you are required to draft.
2. Write down the key facts from the instructions that you feel are relevant to complete your draft, whether you are populating a precedent or amending clauses in a bespoke draft.
3. Check the information in your instructions carefully and then write down the key law or procedure that you think is relevant for you to be able to draft accurately.
4. Check that the law identified in point 3 above relates back to and answers the question(s) you identified in point 1.
5. Structure your draft around those key facts and legal issues, using the template if one is provided.
6. Complete your draft.
7. Review your answer, keeping in mind the SQE2 legal drafting assessment criteria.

Assessment technique

You may be asked to populate a form or a template in the SQE2 drafting assessment, and the key to success here is to combine speed with accuracy. Make sure that you deal with every relevant fact or legal issue, especially if this includes numbers and figures relating to assets and/or inheritance tax; cross-reference the information presented in the documents when drawing up your draft, as this will prevent you from omitting important details. Remember to review your draft to check that it is accurate and comprehensive.

When drafting a more substantial document such as a will, you will need to develop clear, concise and precise language skills for writing the clauses. You will also need to follow the relevant practice principles and formalities, for example not including full stops to avoid the will being fraudulently altered.

SQE2 legal drafting assessment criteria

Try to remember these points as you construct your response, and refer back to them as you review our sample answers in this chapter:

Skills

1. Use clear, precise, concise and acceptable language.
2. Structure the document appropriately and logically.

Application of law

3. Draft a document which is legally correct.
4. Draft a document which is legally comprehensive.
5. Identify any ethical and professional conduct issues and exercise judgement to resolve them honestly and with integrity.

For more support and guidance on how to meet the SQE2 legal drafting assessment criteria, see ***Introduction to Written Legal Skills for SQE2***, chapter 4, Legal drafting.

In ***Revise SQE: Wills and the Administration of Estates***, chapters 1, 3 and 4, we considered the rules relating to revoking a valid will or amending its clauses. Question 1 below demonstrates how your knowledge of this topic could be tested in the context and format of an SQE2 legal drafting in wills assessment.

■ QUESTION 1

Email to candidate

From: Partner
Sent: 13 September 202#
To: Candidate
Subject: Patrick Karman (new will)

We have received instructions from Patrick Karman, who wishes to make a new will with us. He had previously made a will with a different firm of solicitors (**Attachment 1**). Patrick was sent our new will instruction questionnaire and has partially completed it (see **Attachment 2**; Patrick's replies are given in italics and underline). We are awaiting further instructions from Patrick in order to complete this form, and Patrick has promised to send us the additional information shortly.

Patrick lives with his partner, Beth Roper, and Julian, her son from a previous marriage. Patrick has sold the Green Avenue property mentioned in his first will and purchased the property in Cheltenham given as his address in the questionnaire.

Please review the issues arising from Patrick's responses to the instruction questionnaire to draft a new will, using his previous will as a template if appropriate. I have been instructed that the two witnesses remain the same.

Thanks

Partner

Attachments:

1. Patrick Karman's will
2. Will instruction questionnaire

Attachment 1

WILL OF PATRICK KARMAN

I PATRICK KARMAN of 23, Green Avenue, Reddage, BUCKS **HEREBY REVOKE** all former wills and testamentary dispositions made by me **AND DECLARE** this to be my last will and testament

1. **I APPOINT** my sister **JULIE KISSON** of 15, Queen's Lane, Shoreham-by-Sea, West Sussex (hereinafter called 'my Trustee' which expression shall include the trustees or trustee for the time being) to be the executor and trustee of my will
2. **I GIVE** to my sister **JULIE KISSON** named above any interest I may have at the time of my death in 23, Green Avenue, Reddage
3. **I GIVE** to my best friend **DANIEL CRONIN** my **RANGE ROVER SPORT (Registration PAT 1)** or any replacement car I own at my death absolutely and free of tax and costs of transfer
4. **I GIVE** to my friend **WARREN BLACK** the sum of **TEN THOUSAND POUNDS** (£10,000) absolutely and free of tax
5. **I GIVE** to my niece **ARLINE NORMA KISSON** of 15, Queen's Lane, Shoreham-by-Sea, West Sussex the sum of **FIVE THOUSAND POUNDS** (£5,000) absolutely and free of tax

6.1. I **GIVE** to my Executor and Trustee all my real and personal property not hereby nor by any Codicil hereto otherwise disposed of whatsoever and wheresoever (including any property over which I may have a general power of appointment or disposition by Will) (hereafter referred to as 'my Residuary Estate')

6.2. My Executor and Trustee shall pay out of my Residuary Estate my debts, funeral and testamentary expenses and legacies and all inheritance tax

6.3. I give my Residuary Estate to my Trustee to hold on trust for such of my mother **JEMMA KARMAN**

6.4. If the said **JEMMA KARMAN** shall die before me, I give my Residuary Estate to my sister **JULIE KISSON** and her daughter **ARLINE NORMA KISSON**

7. **I DESIRE** that my body be buried at the family plot at Wycombe Cemetery Buckinghamshire
8. The Standard Provisions and all the Special Provisions of the Society of Trust and Estate Practitioners (2nd Edition) shall apply

IN WITNESS whereof I have hereunto set my hand this 14th day of May 2017

SIGNED BY the above named
PATRICK KARMAN

in our joint presence and
then by us in his

} *Patrick Karman*

Mary Peterson

Mary Peterson
2, Market Street
High Wycombe

Clara Burns

Clara Burns
12, Station Parade
Cheltenham

Attachment 2

Bradlings Law LLP 1 High Street Manchester
Will Instruction Questionnaire

Part A: You and your family

1. Your details
Forenames: *Patrick*
Surname: *Karman*
Address: *6 Home Drive, Cheltenham, Gloucestershire GL65 1BA*
Home telephone: *01242 987123*
Business telephone: *01242 123987*
Mobile telephone: *07770 124678*
Date of birth: *2 January 1971*
Occupation: *Builder (self-employed)*

2. Your husband/wife/partner
Forenames: *Beth*
Surname: *Roper*
Date of birth: *19 November 1974*
Occupation: *Professional singer*

3. Marriage/Partnership details
Year of marriage or civil partnership *N/A*

Are you intending to marry/enter into a civil partnership in the near future? *No*

Has either of you been married before? *Yes*

4. Your children (including children from another relationship)
None

5. Children of your husband/wife/partner's previous relationships
Name: *Julian Roper*
Date of birth: *14 October 2004*
Address: *Living with Beth and me at Home Drive*

Part B: Your home and other assets

6. Your home
Is your home owned or rented?
Owned (mortgage-free)

If it is owned, is it in your name alone or jointly with another person?

It is in my name alone

What is the approximate current value of your home?
£510,000

7. Do you have a business?
I am a self-employed builder

8. Your main assets
Please list your other main assets and give approximate values.
- *Gloucester Building Society account no. 88776996 £48,000.00*
- *Santander account no. 12999843 £1,000.00*
- *TSB Bank Current account no. 44657898 £18,000.00*
- *Some shares (£1,000) and insurance policies – details to follow*

9. Joint assets
Please list any jointly owned assets and give approximate values and the name of the other owner.
None

Part C: Funeral, executors and guardians

10. Funeral
Do you wish to be buried, cremated or do you have no preference?
Buried: Cheltenham Cemetery, Church Lane, Cheltenham GL66 5JT

Do you have any other wishes regarding your funeral?
No

11. Executors
My solicitor Jeff Davies to be my executor along with my partner Beth Roper (both also to be trustees)
Jeff Davies, Bradlings LLP, Manchester

12. Guardians
Not appropriate

Part D: Beneficiaries

13. Cash gifts
1. £40,000 to my mother Jemma Karman
2. £10,000 to Arline Norma Kisson my niece (aged 23)

14. Gifts of articles
1. My Range Rover Sport (Registration PAT 1) or any replacement car I own at my death to Julian Roper

2. My shares in GSK (GlaxoSmithKline PLC) (value £1,000) to my sister Julie Kisson, 18, Queen's Lane, Shoreham-by-Sea West Sussex

15. Gifts of residue
All residue, including 6 Home Drive, to my partner Beth Roper

16. Further residuary clause
IF Beth Roper does not survive me or the gift to her fails, I give my residuary estate to Julian Roper

■ YOUR TURN

Have a go at answering question 1, remembering the guidance on pages 82–84.

- Remember the structured approach in the SRA's assessment criteria on page 84.
- Create a list of the most salient legal issues raised by the question, especially the changes to the will as a result of the information in the wills questionnaire.
- Timings are important: you will need to prepare and write your answer in 45 minutes.

SQE1 Functioning legal knowledge link

Remember from ***Revise SQE: Wills and Administration of Estates*** chapters 1, 3 and 4, that changes to a will must be made clearly and accurately. If the contents of a will do not comply with the relevant rules, it is highly likely that part or all of it will be ineffective. If a will fails any of the rules on validity, the probate registry will reject it and the estate will either pass to the personal representatives under an earlier valid will, if there is one, or under the intestacy rules if there is no previous will. A testator can change their mind about a will right up until the moment of death, although the formalities must be observed to make that change of mind effective as an alteration or amendment.

EVALUATING YOUR ANSWER

When you have attempted question 1, mark it yourself against the SQE2 legal drafting assessment criteria. Do you think your attempt met the threshold standard?

Now compare your attempt with the following key legal points and two sample answers to question 1. A circled number indicates that commentary is provided for this part of the answer. The commentary explains whether or not the sample satisfies the assessment criteria, and accordingly whether it is likely to meet the SQE2 threshold standard.

➡Key legal points: question 1

You will need to focus on the following points in order to answer the question:

- If a testator decides to scrap or fundamentally change a will and start again, the Wills Act 1837 sets out the rules for manifesting and communicating that action.
- 'Revocation' occurs when the testator has decided that a previous will they have made should have no effect at all. Although there are exceptions, revocation means that the entire previous will has no effect, and not just parts of it.
- If the testator is generally happy with most of the will but wants to change some minor parts of it or add further dispositions, that will generally be accomplished by making amendments/alterations to the existing will or adding a codicil. Here the information provided in the new wills questionnaire means that changes to many clauses in Patrick's will are required. A new will should therefore be redrafted, albeit using the first will as a template.

■ SAMPLE ANSWER 1 TO QUESTION 1

Please find amendments drafted in underline.

WILL OF PATRICK KARMAN ❶

I PATRICK KARMAN of 6 Home Drive, Cheltenham, Gloucestershire GL65 1BA **HEREBY REVOKE** all former wills and testamentary dispositions made by me **AND DECLARE** this to be my last will and testament ❷

1. **I APPOINT** my partner **BETH ROPER** of 6 Home Drive, Cheltenham, Gloucestershire GL65 1BA, along with my solicitor **JEFF DAVIES** of Bradlings LLP, Manchester (hereinafter called 'my Trustees' which expression shall include the trustees for the time being) to be the executors and trustees of my will ❸

2. **I GIVE** any interest I may have at the time of my death in 6 Home Drive, Cheltenham, Gloucestershire GL65 1BA to my partner **BETH ROPER** named above

3. **I GIVE** my **Range Rover Sport (Registration PAT 1)** or any replacement car I own at my death to **JULIAN ROPER**, absolutely and free of tax and costs of transfer ❹

4. **I GIVE** any shares I own in the company **GlaxoSmithKline PLC** at the date of my death to my sister **JULIE KISSON** of 18, Queen's Lane, Shoreham-by-Sea, West Sussex, absolutely and free of tax and costs of transfer ❺

5. I **GIVE** the sum of **FORTY THOUSAND POUNDS (£40,000)** to my mother **JEMMA KARMAN** absolutely and free of tax and costs of transfer ❻

6. **I GIVE** the sum of **TEN THOUSAND POUNDS (£10,000)** to my niece **ARLINE NORMA KISSON** of 18, Queen's Lane, Shoreham-by-Sea, West Sussex absolutely and free of tax ❼

7.1. **I GIVE** to my Executors and Trustees all my real and personal property not hereby nor by any Codicil hereto otherwise disposed of whatsoever and wheresoever (including any property over which I may have a general power of appointment or disposition by Will) (hereafter referred to as 'my Residuary Estate')

7.2. My Executors and Trustees shall pay out of my Residuary Estate my debts, funeral and testamentary expenses and legacies and all inheritance tax

7.3. My Executors and Trustees shall hold the remainder of my Residuary Estate for my partner **BETH ROPER** absolutely if she survives me by twenty-eight days whether or not she proves this will

7.4. IF the said **BETH ROPER** does not survive me by twenty-eight days or the gift to her fails for any other reason, I give my Residuary Estate to **JULIAN ROPER** ❽

8. **I DESIRE** that my body be buried at Cheltenham Cemetery, Church Lane, Cheltenham GL65 5JT ❾

9. The Standard Provisions and all the Special Provisions of the Society of Trust and Estate Practitioners (2nd Edition) shall apply

IN WITNESS whereof I have hereunto set my hand this [date]

SIGNED BY the above named PATRICK KARMAN in our joint presence and then by us in his	Patrick Karman

Mary Peterson
2, Market Street
High Wycombe

Clara Burns
12, Station Parade
Cheltenham ❿

COMMENTARY

❶ This is a good start. The candidate has assessed the number of changes to the will and has decided to use the previous will as a template for redrafting. This satisfies the assessment criteria for structuring the draft appropriately and logically.

❷ The candidate has spotted the first change required by the questionnaire – the new address. In your SQE2 assessment, make sure that you read the details carefully so that you manage all changes to the new draft effectively. Here the candidate amends the will accurately.

❸ In the original will there is only one executor and trustee, which is Patrick's sister. The instructions require two new executors, Beth and Jeff, and the candidate does well to make the changes without changing the overall structure of the will. The detail is clear and the addresses are also added accurately. The candidate has reviewed their work carefully and amended the text to ensure that plural forms are correctly added to the nouns, trustee and executor. This use of precise language satisfies the assessment criteria.

❹ The candidate has correctly inputted Patrick's partner as beneficiary of the property in clause 2, in place of his sister in the original will. They have also realised that Julian is now to receive Patrick's car; this has again been managed successfully and details of the new car set down. The candidate has worked out that Julian is already of age (over 21 years old) and has correctly excluded any 'trust' element the gift of the car. Note also that the candidate has reordered all the specific legacies so that the legacy is described first and the legatee afterwards. This is in line with usual professional practice and demonstrates excellent skills relating to appropriate structure and clarity.

❺ The candidate has effectively introduced a new clause (4) to deal with the legacy to his sister of the named shares. Although the questionnaire states that the value of the shares is £1,000, the candidate has accounted for the possibility of the testator having more than £1,000 worth of shares in the company at their date of death. This shows good practice, and allows the draft to be legally correct and comprehensive as required by the assessment criteria.

6 In clause 5 the candidate has changed the pecuniary legacy to Warren Black in the first will in favour of Patrick's mother. They have noted the fact that his mother is no longer the residual legatee but rather has a new gift of £40,000, and they have correctly drafted this new clause with clarity. These details were hidden within the questionnaire and could be easily overlooked. The candidate has also picked up on the change of address for Patrick's sister on the questionnaire, who has moved from 15 Queen's Lane to number 18. This shows close attention to detail.

7 The candidate corrects the pecuniary legacy to his niece from £5,000 to £10,000 and accurately adds the correct details in relation to his niece and her address.

8 In conclusion the candidate accurately amends clause 6 of the first will. As noted in point 3 above, the correct plural forms are added to clauses 7.1–7.3 to reflect the new executors. In clause 7.3 the candidate has made Beth the residuary legatee to reflect item 15 of the questionnaire, and added a further residue clause in favour of Julian at 7.4 to address the new instruction in item 16 of the questionnaire. It is extremely pleasing to see that other assets are not added to the will specifically (the bank accounts, for example). There are no specific gifts of this money in the questionnaire so these would fall into residue automatically. The candidate has dealt with this effectively here.

9 The candidate has correctly completed another change required by the questionnaire - the burial instructions and change of venue. It would be easy to miss these details whilst focusing on the main clauses of the will. When you have completed your draft in the SQE2 assessment, check your work carefully against the materials provided to ensure that you have made all of the required changes.

10 The candidate has correctly copied the details of the witnesses from the first will, in line with the instructions that the same witnesses will be used again.

Does this answer meet the threshold?

The sample answer contains all of the information relating to the new will that the client requires and that the candidate has been asked to provide. This is a very sound effort: the candidate has implemented all of the relevant changes to the will, both major and minor, thus demonstrating to the assessor their ability to undertake a close reading of the materials and apply their legal knowledge when drafting a new will. They have produced an accurate, legally correct will with the relevant formalities. In practice this new will must be signed and witnessed following the procedure laid out in the Wills Act 1837, taking care not to allow a beneficiary to act as a witness to the will. This new draft is suitable for that next stage, so it is highly likely that this attempt would pass the SQE2 standard threshold.

Now consider the second sample answer to question 1.

■ SAMPLE ANSWER 2 TO QUESTION 1

Please find amendments drafted in underline.

WILL OF PATRICK CARMAN ❶

I PATRICK KARMAN of 6 Hole Drive, Cheltenham, Gloucestershire GL56 1BA **HEREBY REVOKE** all former wills and testamentary dispositions made by me **AND DECLARE** this to be my last will and testament ❷

1. **I APPOINT** my partner **BETH ROPER** of 6 Home Drive, Cheltenham, Gloucestershire GL65 1BA, along with my solicitor **JEFF DAVIES** of Bradlings LLP, Manchester as the trustees of my will ❸
2. **I GIVE** to my partner **BETH ROPER** named above any interest I may have at the time of my death in 6 Home Drive, Cheltenham, Gloucestershire GL65 1BA ❹
3. **I GIVE** to **JULIAN ROPER** my car, or leave my car on trust to my executors to be held for Julian should he not be of age at my death absolutely and free of tax and costs of transfer ❺
4. **I GIVE** to **JULIE** my shares of **ONE THOUSAND POUNDS (£1,000)** absolutely and free of tax and costs of transfer ❻
5. I **GIVE** to my mother **JEMMA KARMAN** the sum of **£40,000 (FORTY THOUSAND POUNDS)** if I should predecease her absolutely and free of tax and costs of transfer and also **GIVE** to my friend **WARREN BLACK** the sum of **£10,000 (TEN THOUSAND POUNDS)** absolutely and free of tax and costs of transfer ❼
6. **I GIVE** to my niece **ARLINE NORMA KISSON** of 15, Queen's Lane, Shoreham-by-Sea, West Sussex the sum of **FIVE THOUSAND POUNDS** (£5,000) absolutely and free of tax ❽

7.1. **I GIVE** to my Executor and Trustee all my real and personal property not hereby nor by any Codicil hereto otherwise disposed of whatsoever and wheresoever (including any property over which I may have a general power of appointment or disposition by Will) (hereafter referred to as 'my Residuary Estate')

7.2. My Executor and Trustee shall pay out of my Residuary Estate my debts, funeral and testamentary expenses and legacies and all inheritance tax

7.3. My Executor and Trustee shall hold the remainder of my Residuary Estate for my partner **BETH ROPER** (if I predecease her) along with the money in my bank accounts ❾

8. **I DESIRE** that my body be buried at the family plot at Wycombe Cemetery Buckinghamshire ❿

9. The Standard Provisions and all the Special Provisions of the Society of Trust and Estate Practitioners (2nd Edition) shall apply

IN WITNESS whereof I have hereunto set my hand this [date]

SIGNED BY the above named
PATRICK KARMAN

in our joint presence and
then by us in his

} Patrick Karman

Mary Peterson

2, Market Street
High Wycombe ⓫

COMMENTARY

❶ This is not a great start. The matter is identified but the name of the client is inaccurately spelled with an initial C rather than a K. This does not demonstrate attention to detail and lacks professionalism. It may also have consequences later if the will is challenged. This is a professional conduct issue and would not satisfy the assessment criteria. As in sample answer 1, this candidate has also used the previous will as a template. This indicates good structure, but here the candidate has not been careful enough in updating all of the clauses.

❷ The candidate seems to suffer here from a lack of accuracy once again: in the address they have written 'Hole' instead of 'Home' and inserted the new postcode incorrectly - GL56 instead of GL65. This again lacks professionalism and attention to detail, meaning that the drafting is not client-focused.

❸ Although the details are accurate here, the candidate has made a potentially fatal error in naming Beth and Jeff as trustees only and failing to name them as executors. Without named executors, the will may be argued to be incomplete. Administrators may need to be appointed after the fact, which could cause delay and confusion. It is well established that executors may also be named as trustees, but if there are no named executors the client (through their solicitor) will need to rely on implied executorship. This is never good practice.

❹ Clause 2 has been accurately amended from the first will, to install Beth as the beneficiary of the house. Notice however that, here and in the other clauses, the candidate follows the order of the first will in placing the legatee first and then the legacy, which is not the best practice when drafting a will.

❺ The candidate uses vague language in this clause. They simply list 'my car' as a legacy. This could cause a problem later because it may be unclear as to which car: the car at the time of writing the will or a car existing at the time of death? The candidate should have clarified the drafting here, to suggest the actual car or at the least a substitute at the time of death if different. The wording here is also rather vague, as there is a mention of 'my executors' here without having named them in an earlier clause. This clause drafting does not therefore meet the assessment criteria's requirement for clear, precise, concise and appropriate language. There is also no need to refer to the 'trust' element here - the candidate has missed the fact that Julian is already over the age of 21 at the time of the new will. There is a further error, in that the gift should not be left to executors to pass on: it would always be gifted to trustees to hold on trust for any beneficiaries.

6 The candidate correctly creates a new clause to include the legacy of shares for the client's sister. However, this clause is not complete or accurate, as it names 'Julie' but does not provide her full name or address. This could cause problems later if the will is challenged on account of the uncertainty of the legatee's identity. The shares are also not named as being GlaxoSmithKline PLC shares as per the questionnaire, and the candidate has not accounted for the value of the shares to be greater than the amount specified in the questionnaire. This will not be a legally comprehensive draft, as required by the assessment criteria.

7 The candidate deals with the legacy for his mother accurately but does not remove the legacy for his friend Warren from the original will, instead including both gifts in the same clause. This again is inaccurate and does not demonstrate a client-focused approach. Such an error would directly affect Beth by reducing the money falling into the residue.

8 The candidate does not amend clause 5 of the original will, thereby making the mistakes of leaving the legacy to his niece as £5,000 instead of amending to £10,000 and not marking the legatee's change of address.

9 In clauses 7.1–7.3, the candidate inaccurately retains the singular form for executor and trustee, more examples of inattention to detail. In clause 7.3, there is no need to make this vague reference to the money in the bank accounts as this is residue in any case rather than a specific legacy. Finally, the candidate has missed the further residue clause in the questionnaire in favour of Julian, and so this point is not covered or included in the new will.

10 The candidate has not noticed the change of address for burial as provided in the questionnaire. Once again this demonstrates a lack of care and diligence to the SQE2 assessor, and in practice could cause problems for Patrick's family in the future, after his death.

11 The candidate has only copied the details of one witness from the original will, although the instructions stated that both would be used again.

Does this answer meet the threshold?

When assessing the second written response against the SQE2 legal drafting assessment criteria, it is unlikely that it would meet the threshold standard. The candidate has misinterpreted or misapplied the instructions and legacies and made errors in relation to the distribution of assets and naming the executors. The drafting is vague and inaccurate, and does not show full understanding of how the information in the questionnaire should affect the drafting of the new will. This response serves as a reminder of how important it is to read through all materials carefully: details contained in the questionnaire were missed by this candidate, with serious consequences for the client and their will.

The SQE2 assessment can focus on any area of the SQE1 specification. Below is an example of how different parts of the specification – affidavits of search and due execution when applying for probate – could arise in the context of SQE2 legal drafting in wills.

■ QUESTION 2

Email to candidate

From: Partner
Sent: 13 November 202#
To: Candidate
Subject: Erwin Charles (Dawn Charles deceased)

I have spoken this morning to a new client, Mr Erwin Charles. His wife, Dawn, recently died, and, although Erwin says that she wrote a will, it cannot be found. The couple moved house a year before Dawn died, and Erwin thinks that the will was lost in the move. He has contacted their previous solicitor, Tara Neville, Dawn's best friend, Norma Smurkitt, and the only surviving member of Dawn's family, her distant aunt Ginny Lyons. None of these contacts were able to help. The firm has been asked to draft an affidavit of search to assist in a possible application for grant of letters of administration to the Nottingham Registry. A template is enclosed as **Attachment 1**.

According to Erwin, Dawn spoke to him about her will just weeks before she died, saying that she hoped he would follow her instructions 'should the worst happen' as one of her executors. Erwin has also told us that he has a relevant witness who can confirm that the original will was valid in relation to the necessary formalities. The couple had no children, siblings, parents or any family members other than Ginny. Please see the handwritten note from one of the potential witnesses in **Exhibit A** (**Attachment 2**) that Erwin has presented. It attests to the fact that an original will was signed and dated 5 May 2014, and that two named witnesses signed the will (one of which is the author of the note). The note confirms that the intended executors were Erwin and Norma, and that Erwin was the sole beneficiary. To assist us in applying for probate, we need to draft an affidavit of due execution using the template in **Attachment 3**.

Here is the information as supplied by Erwin in this morning's meeting:
- Dawn died intestate (as there is no valid will) without leaving any issue, on 20 October 202#.
- Her address at time of death was the marital home shared with Erwin Charles: 1 St John's Avenue, Mattersley, Nottingham NG37 4LP.
- Dawn had no debts. You do not need to deal with inheritance tax and other estate administration expenses.

Please complete the following tasks:
1. **Draft the template affidavit of search as Mr Charles will wish to apply for letters of administration.**
2. **Draft the affidavit of due execution, ready to be approved and signed by the witness who provided the handwritten note.**

Thanks

Partner

Attachments:
1. Affidavit of search template
2. Exhibit A: letter from Annette Lewis
3. Affidavit of due execution template

Attachment 1

Affidavit of search template

In the High Court of Justice
Family Division
The [Principal OR [name] District Probate] Registry at [placename]

In the estate of [name] deceased

I [full true name, full permanent address and occupation, or if no occupation a description, of deponent or witness] make [oath and say that OR the following statement]:

1. I am [the sole executor OR the surviving executor OR one of the executors] named in the last will and testament of [full true name of deceased] [otherwise known as [alternative/alias name of deceased]] of [full private permanent address] deceased the will [bearing date [date] OR being undated] being now produced [to OR by] me and marked ['A'].
2. Referring to the fact that [specify reason why there is doubt as to whether the will sought to be proved is the last will of the deceased] I have made all possible searches and enquiries for any other will including a search of the home of the deceased and of all places where it is likely that they kept their important papers or valuable personal belongings.
3. I have been unable to discover any testamentary document other than [the will, or other document].
4. I have made enquiries of [specify persons of whom enquiries have been made, such as solicitor, bank manager, accountant or relatives] in an effort to trace any other testamentary document.
5. I believe the deceased died without having left any will or other testamentary document other than the will referred to above.

Statement of truth

I believe that the facts stated in this witness statement are true and understand that criminal proceedings for fraud may be brought against me if I am found to have been deliberately untruthful or dishonest.

Signed: [signature]

Dated: [date]

Attachment 2

Exhibit A

14 New Bosworth Road
Nottingham
NG37 2EL
5th November 202#

Dear Erwin.

Firstly, may I just send you my heartfelt condolences on the passing of Dawn. She was such a dear friend and I will miss her terribly, especially now that I am retired and would have had more time to see Dawn.

From our telephone call last week, I understand that you cannot find a will. I am more than happy to sign a formal statement to confirm that I saw Dawn sign a will, and according to my records this was on 5th May 2014. I was one of Dawn's witnesses along with her work colleague at that time who I believe was called Ray Wise (but I'm afraid I don't have any other details about him). I can confirm that Ray and I witnessed Dawn signing the will and we also both signed as witnesses together – all three of us signed at the same time on 5th May.

I can also confirm to the best of my knowledge and memory that you were her sole beneficiary as I remember her telling us that there was 'no one else'. I remember that you and Norma [Smurkitt] were down to be the executors of the will as Dawn told me that she didn't trust anyone else.

I hope that helps and let me know if I need to do anything else.

Warm wishes and deepest sympathy again

Annette [Lewis]

Attachment 3

Affidavit of due execution template

In the High Court of Justice
Family Division [Probate]

In the Estate of [full name of deceased], Deceased

I, [your full name], of [your full home address], [your occupation], will say as follows:

1. I am one of the subscribing witnesses to the last Will and Testament of [name of deceased], late of [deceased's last address], deceased.
2. The said Will is dated [date of will] and is now produced and shown to me marked 'Exhibit A'.
3. On [date the will was signed], the deceased executed the said Will by signing their name at the foot or end of it in the presence of myself and [name of second witness], both of us being present at the same time.
4. We, the said [your name] and [second witness name], then and there attested and subscribed the said Will in the presence of the deceased.

5. *Optional: Add details if the Will was signed by someone else at the deceased's direction or if there were specific circumstances such as a 'video-witnessed' Will.]*

Statement of truth

I believe that the facts stated in this witness statement are true. I understand that proceedings for contempt of court may be brought against anyone who makes, or causes to be made, a false statement in a document verified by a statement of truth without an honest belief in its truth.

Signed:

Name: [your printed name]

Dated: [current date]

* * *

■ YOUR TURN

Have a go at answering question 2, remembering the guidance on pages 82-84.

- Remember the structured approach in the SRA's assessment criteria earlier in the chapter.
- Create a list of the most salient legal issues raised by the question, especially the value of the assets.
- Timings are important: you will need to prepare and write your answer in 45 minutes.

SQE1 Functioning legal knowledge link

Remember from ***Revise SQE: Wills and Administration of Estates***, chapter 7, that there is both law and process when drafting an affidavit of search or of due execution. The necessary formalities must be followed, and drafting must be precise and accurate.

EVALUATING YOUR ANSWER

When you have attempted question 2, mark it yourself against the SQE2 legal drafting assessment criteria. Do you think your attempt met the threshold standard?

Now compare your attempt with the following key legal points and two sample answers to question 2. A circled number indicates that commentary is provided for this part of the answer. The commentary explains whether or not the sample satisfies the assessment criteria, and accordingly whether it is likely to meet the SQE2 threshold standard.

➡Key legal points: question 2

- If a valid will has been left and the deceased has therefore died testate, the executors should seek a grant of probate. If no valid will has been left, there is a full intestacy and the appropriate administrators must apply for a grant of letters of administration. However, it may be that an original will was lost, as in this case.
- If there is a valid will but no executor able or willing to act, then the person entitled to be an administrator must apply for a grant of letters of administration with the

will annexed. But, where there is no original will, an affidavit of search needs to be submitted with the application for grant. If this is not accepted, then intestacy rules apply after a grant of administration. In this question, an affidavit of due execution must also be drafted, as there is a witness who can attest to the validity of the will.

- The aim of an affidavit of search is to convince probate that there was an original will, and rebut the presumption that the original will was revoked. The affidavit must therefore give details of a thorough search for the will, offering reasons why it has been lost if possible.
- It may be necessary to include an affidavit of due execution where there is a witness who can attest to the will being created, as we have on the facts of this case.

SAMPLE ANSWER 1 TO QUESTION 2

Please find amendments drafted in bold.

Affidavit of search

In the High Court of Justice
Family Division
The **District Probate** Registry at **Nottingham**

In the estate of **DAWN CHARLES** deceased

I ERWIN CHARLES, of 1 St JOHN'S AVENUE, MATTERSLEY, NOTTINGHAM, NOTTINGHAMSHIRE, NG37 4LP, husband of Dawn Charles, make the following statement: ❶

1. I am **one of the executors** named in the last will and testament of **DAWN CHARLES** of **1 ST JOHN'S AVENUE, MATTERSLEY, NOTTINGHAM, NOTTINGHAMSHIRE, NG37 4LP** deceased the original will bearing **date 5th May 2014, which is lost, but there is a handwritten note attesting to due execution dated 5th November 202#** being now produced **by** me and marked **Exhibit A.** ❷
2. Referring to the fact that **the original copy of the will is lost, due to it being misplaced during a property move approximately one year before Dawn Charles's death, and due to the fact that there is no reason to believe the original will was revoked, evidenced by the fact that in the weeks before her death Dawn Charles discussed the original will with me, stating that she hoped I would follow her instructions 'should the worst happen' as one of her executors, and the facts given in the handwritten note (Exhibit A),** I have made all possible searches and enquiries for any other will including a search of the home of the deceased and of all places where it is likely that they kept their important papers or valuable personal belongings. ❸
3. I have been unable to discover any testamentary document other than **Exhibit A. This is a handwritten note which Mrs Annette Lewis, one of the witnesses to the original will, sent to me after my wife passed away. The note is dated 5th November 202# and attests to the facts that the original will was signed by the testator and two witnesses, the intended executors were myself and Norma Smurkitt, and I was to be the sole beneficiary.** ❹
4. I have made enquiries of **our previous solicitor, Tara Neville, and also contacted Dawn's best friend Norma Smurkitt, as well as the only surviving member of Dawn's family, her aunt Ginny Lyons. None of these contacts was able to help** in an effort to trace any other testamentary document. ❺

5. I believe the deceased died without having left any will or other testamentary document other than the will **referred to as Exhibit A**. ❻

I believe that the facts stated in this witness statement are true. I understand that proceedings for contempt of court may be brought against anyone who makes, or causes to be made, a false statement in a document verified by a statement of truth without an honest belief in its truth.

Signed: **Erwin Charles**

Dated: **[current date]** ❼

Affidavit of due execution

In the High Court of Justice
Family Division
The District Probate Registry at Nottingham

In the estate of **Dawn Charles**, Deceased

I, **Annette Lewis**, of **14 New Bosworth Road, Nottingham, NG37 2EL**, **retired**, will say as follows: ❽

1. I am one of the subscribing witnesses to the last Will and Testament of **Dawn Charles**, late of **1, St John's Avenue, Mattersley, Nottingham, Nottinghamshire, NG37 4LP**, deceased.
2. The said Will is dated **5th May 2014, which I understand is lost, but is referred to in my handwritten note dated 5th November 202# which** is now produced and shown to me marked 'Exhibit A'. ❾
3. On **5th May 2014**, the deceased executed the said Will by signing their name at the foot or end of it in the presence of myself and **Ray Wise**, both of us being present at the same time.
4. We, the said **Annette Lewis** and **Ray Wise**, then and there attested and subscribed the said Will in the presence of the deceased.
5. **I can attest to the fact the original will was signed by the testator and the said two witnesses and showed the intended executors as Erwin Charles and Norma Smurkitt with Erwin Charles as sole beneficiary.** ❿

Statement of truth

I believe that the facts stated in this witness statement are true. I understand that proceedings for contempt of court may be brought against anyone who makes, or causes to be made, a false statement in a document verified by a statement of truth without an honest belief in its truth.

Signed:

Name: Annette Lewis

Date: [current date] ⓫

COMMENTARY

❶ The candidate begins strongly by including the reference to the district registry in Nottingham where Dawn and Erwin were domiciled and inserting the correct name and address of the client, Erwin Charles. This shows a careful eye for detail, which continues throughout the answer. A quick glance at the whole document also reveals that the candidate has correctly followed the template provided, which demonstrates to the assessor that this draft is well structured.

❷ The candidate accurately refers to the original will and the handwritten note in the attached documents. This is an appropriately brief and clear explanation of the lost will and reason for the handwritten note, and the candidate uses the correct dates to signpost the assessor to the relevant documents. This prepares the reader for the next clause and demonstrates sound professional practice skills.

❸ The candidate has given accurate details as to the basis of the affidavit, especially in relation to the reason why the will was lost, and that there was a handwritten note that will be used to form the basis of the evidence for the affidavit of due execution. Most importantly, evidence to rebut the presumption of revocation of the original will is present and clearly explained (vital in an affidavit of this nature). The candidate has reproduced the correct parts of the accompanying documents to provide this explanation and demonstrates a close eye for detail.

❹ Once again, accurate details are provided here in relation to the search and to the fact that a witness is available who can attest to the original will evidenced by her handwritten note. Without reference to the note there would be no evidence, and this could be a professional conduct issue.

❺ There is clear reference to the search efforts, naming individuals who have been contacted. This is a key requirement of this document, and this response demonstrates the candidate's legal knowledge and accurate skills in drafting this document.

❻ The candidate confirms again that the handwritten note is the evidence required for this affidavit.

❼ The candidate does not need to add anything else to the end of the document: this is an accurate statement of truth and demonstrates sound professional conduct in its drafting. The candidate has correctly prepared the end of the document for signing and dating by the client.

❽ In the second drafting task, the affidavit of due execution, the candidate immediately demonstrates accurate use of the materials by adding the same probate registry in Nottingham as with the affidavit of search. The candidate has used the correct name and address of the witness, and also found the reference to the witness's occupation as 'retired' from the handwritten note.

❾ The candidate has accurately referred to the original will and correct date, and also references the handwritten note, its date and exhibit number. This is key evidence: the registry would be unlikely to allow this application without the affidavit of due execution and the note, and this is an excellent demonstration of accuracy and attention to detail.

❿ The candidate takes the opportunity to write a new clause 5, explaining the witnessing of the original will and the correct details of the proposed executors, as well as a clear assertion that no one else is to lose any beneficial entitlement if intestacy rules are applied as Erwin is the sole beneficiary.

⓫ The statement of truth is correctly presented at the end of this affidavit, and the candidate has prepared the end of the document for signing and dating. This draft shows attention to detail and excellent professional practice.

Does this answer meet the threshold?

The sample answer contains all of the information and application of the facts and legal requirements relating to the drafting of both affidavits. The drafts satisfy the relevant formalities and are accurate in terms of the parties, the details of the lost original will and the evidence of due execution. Both affidavits are clear, succinct and legally correct, and written with the appropriate style and format. There is a thorough explanation of how and why the original will was lost, and at all times the drafts are client-focused and relevant. This response is therefore likely to meet the threshold standard for SQE2 legal drafting.

Now consider the second sample answer to question 2.

■ SAMPLE ANSWER 2 TO QUESTION 2

Affidavit of search

In the High Court of Justice
Family Division
The District Probate Registry ❶

In the estate of **DAWN CHARLES** deceased

I ERWIN CHARLES, of 1 ST JOHN'S AVENUE, MATTERSLEY, NOTTINGHAM, NOTTINGHAMSHIRE, NG37 4LP, husband of Dawn Charles, make the following statement:

1. I am **the executor** named in the last will and testament of **DAWN CHARLES** of **1 ST JOHN'S AVENUE, MATTERSLEY, NOTTINGHAM, NOTTINGHAMSHIRE, NG37 4LP** deceased the original will bearing date **5th May 2014, which is lost, but there is handwritten note attesting to due execution being now produced by me.** ❷
2. Referring to the fact that **the original copy of the will is lost, and due to the fact that there is no reason to believe the original will was revoked, evidenced by the fact that Dawn Charles discussed the original will with me, and the facts given in the handwritten note,** I have made all possible searches and enquiries for any other will including a search of the home of the deceased and of all places where it is likely that they kept their important papers or valuable personal belongings. ❸
3. I have been unable to discover any testamentary document other than **a handwritten note from one of the witnesses to the original will, Mrs Annette Lewis, who sent me this note recently. The note suggests that the will was signed by the testator and two witnesses and shows the intended executors as myself and Norma Smurfitt.** ❹
4. I have made enquiries of **many contacts including our previous solicitor, and friends and family members of Dawn. None of these contacts were able to help** in an effort to trace any other testamentary document. ❺
5. I believe the deceased died without having left any will or other testamentary document other than the will referred to **in the note**.

I believe that the facts stated in this witness statement are true. ❻

Signed: Erwin Charles

Dated: [today's date]

Affidavit of due execution

In the High Court of Justice
Family Division
The District Probate Registry

In the Estate of **Dawn Charles**, Deceased

I, **Annette Lewis**, of **14 New Bosworth Road, Nottingham, NG37 2EL**, will say as follows: ❼

1. I am one of the subscribing witnesses to the last Will and Testament of **Dawn Charles**, late of **1, St John's Avenue, Mattersley, Nottingham, Nottinghamshire, NG37 4LP**, deceased.
2. The said Will is **lost, but is referred to in my handwritten note** and is now produced and shown to me marked **'Exhibit A'**. ❽
3. On **5th May 2014**, the deceased executed the said Will by signing their name at the foot or end of it in the presence of myself, being present at the time.
4. **I**, the said **Annette Lewis**, then and there attested and subscribed the said Will in the presence of the deceased. ❾
5. **I can attest to the fact the original will was signed showing the intended executors as Erwin Charles and Norma Smurkitt.** ❿

Statement of truth

I believe that the facts stated in this witness statement are true. I understand that proceedings for contempt of court may be brought against anyone who makes, or causes to be made, a false statement in a document verified by a statement of truth without an honest belief in its truth.

Signed: Annette Lewis ⓫

Name: Annette Lewis

Dated: [current date]

COMMENTARY

❶ The candidate begins weakly by omitting reference to the specific district registry in Nottingham. This shows a lack of diligence and professional care and suggests that the candidate has rushed on to the main body of the draft. Remember to consider and amend all editable elements of a draft, to produce a comprehensive document.

❷ The format of the template is followed correctly, demonstrating appropriate and logical structure. However, the candidate fails to provide specific detail in relation to the handwritten note, such as the date and exhibit number. They also state that Erwin Charles is 'the executor', omitting to mention that Norma is also an executor. This inaccurate drafting is a professional conduct issue.

❸ The candidate does not give accurate details for the basis of the affidavit, especially in relation to the reason why the will was lost. More details about the handwritten note are also required, as this will form the basis of the evidence for the affidavit of due execution. Most importantly, evidence to rebut the presumption of revocation of the original will is not present and not clearly explained. This draft will not be legally comprehensive, and as such will not satisfy the assessment criteria.

❹ Once again, there is insufficient detail of the search for the will and the existence of the note. The candidate fails to give the date of the note and when it was sent to him, and also misspells the name of the second executor, writing 'Smurfitt' instead of 'Smurkitt'. There is also a contradiction here with clause 1, which states that Erwin was 'the' executor. The candidate omits to include that according to the note Erwin is the sole beneficiary, which is a vital point in the argument that intestacy would make no difference to the outcome of the distribution of assets. Without accurate reference to the note there is no evidence, and this could be a professional conduct issue.

5. The candidate does not make clear reference to the search efforts and fails to name individuals who have been contacted. This is a key requirement and demonstrates a lack of legal knowledge and drafting accuracy.
6. Finally, this is not a complete statement of truth. As such, the candidate fails to demonstrate sound professional conduct.
7. In the second drafting task, the affidavit of due execution, the candidate has again missed the opportunity to identify the probate registry in Nottingham as the correct registry. They have included the correct name and address of the witness but have not inferred the witness's retirement status from the handwritten note. These errors mean that, right from the start, the assessor will be able to see that this is not a legally comprehensive draft.
8. The candidate does not refer accurately to the correct date of the original will or to the date and exhibit number of the handwritten note. The note is key evidence for the registry, and the candidate is demonstrating a casual approach to detail here.
9. In clauses 3 and 4, the explanation of the witnessing of the original will is vague, and the candidate entirely omits details of the second witness, Ray Wise. This oversight adds to the draft's lack of comprehensiveness and the candidate's inability to produce an accurate and precise document.
10. The candidate makes good use of the option to add a clause 5, but here too there is a lack of clarity: they do not say that the will was signed by the testator or that Erwin was beneficiary.
11. The candidate has added Annette's name to the signature line, but this should have been left blank.

Does this answer meet the threshold?

When assessing the second draft against the SQE2 legal drafting assessment criteria, it is unlikely that it would meet the threshold standard. The candidate has misapplied the material, omitted vital details and made many errors, especially in relation to the names and even existence of key parties. This fails to demonstrate the candidate's ability to draft with accuracy and attention to detail and shows a lack of legal knowledge about what is needed in a sound affidavit for a successful application to the probate registry.

■ KEY POINT CHECKLIST

This chapter has covered the following key knowledge points:

- The SQE2 assessment criteria for legal drafting and how to apply them in the context of wills and the administration of estates.
- A suggested structure for approaching an SQE2 legal drafting question.
- Examples of legal drafting that are likely and unlikely to meet the threshold standard, with full commentary on their strengths and weaknesses.

■ SUMMARY AND REFLECTION

When approaching the SQE2 drafting assessment, take plenty of time to read the question carefully. Think about the legal and procedural points the question is asking of you and highlight the key details in the materials that will affect your drafting of the document. If a template is provided, follow this closely so that your draft is appropriately and logically structured.

The assessor will be judging your ability to draft both correctly and comprehensively, so, as well as pinpointing any relevant law, you will need to demonstrate how it can be applied to the wider context of the client's scenario. Use clear, concise and acceptable language whilst writing your draft, and fill in forms with detail and precision. When approaching a drafting task on the topic of wills, it is especially important that you transfer the correct names, addresses and dates onto your draft.

Now take time to reflect and consider what you might still need to work on, and whether you feel completely confident in your legal drafting skills in the context of wills and the administration of estates.

FINAL WORDS

We hope that the guidance and examples contained in this book have helped to put into context how to use your practice skills to ensure you reach the SQE2 grading criteria. Remember, above all, that this is an assessment, and the assessor needs to see evidence that you have met the criteria in order for you to pass the threshold. Always keep this in the back of your mind when taking your SQE2 assessments.

Whilst this book is designed to aid your learning and provide helpful tips on how to pass your SQE2 assessments, it is no substitute for practice. All skills are improved with repetition and refining your technique, and legal skills are no exception to this rule. Take any opportunity you can to write letters, draft legal documents and practise your interviewing and advocacy skills. Reflect carefully on your performance after each exercise:

- What could you have done better?
- Did you meet all of the grading criteria applicable to that particular skill?
- Do you need to fill any gaps in your legal knowledge?

Constant practice and self-reflection are the keys to success.

Finally, the team at *Revise SQE* wish you the best of luck in your SQE2 assessments!

Appendix

PERFORMANCE INDICATORS FOR SQE2 CASE AND MATTER ANALYSIS ASSESSMENT CRITERIA

Skills	*Indicators demonstrating competence*	*Indicators that do not demonstrate competence*
Identify relevant facts	• The candidate selects facts that are important in ensuring the client's needs/objectives are met, or are relevant to the legal analysis, from the documentation provided	• The candidate refers to all facts from the documentation, regardless of whether or not they are important in meeting the client's objectives or relevant to their legal analysis • The candidate refers only to irrelevant facts • The candidate does not refer to sufficient relevant facts to support the legal analysis
Provide client-focused advice (ie advice which demonstrates an understanding of the problem from the client's point of view and what the client wants to achieve, not just from a legal perspective)	• The candidate demonstrates an understanding of the client's problem from the client's perspective • The candidate addresses the client's legal problem, any relevant commercial considerations and/or the client's personal circumstances, priorities, objectives and constraints	• The candidate does not approach or appreciate the client's problem from the client's perspective • The candidate does not focus on the issues identified by the client
Use clear, precise, concise and acceptable language	• The reader understands the candidate's use of language and clarity of expression • The candidate avoids unnecessary technical terms/legal jargon	• The reader struggles to understand the candidate's use of language; the answer lacks clarity and/or is poorly expressed • The reader's understanding is adversely affected by the density, length or brevity of the answer • The candidate uses unnecessary technical terms/legal jargon

Law	*Indicators demonstrating competence*	*Indicators that do not demonstrate competence*
Apply the law correctly to the client's situation	• The candidate identifies the relevant fundamental legal principles in accordance with the SQE2 assessment specification and applies them correctly to the facts of the client's case	• The candidate does not identify and correctly apply the relevant legal principles to the facts of the client's case • The candidate does not apply the relevant legal principles in a way that addresses the client's needs and concerns
Apply the law comprehensively to the client's situation	• The candidate's legal analysis is sufficiently detailed in the context of the client's case, eg assessing information to identify key issues and risks; reaching reasonable conclusions supported by relevant evidence	• The candidate's legal analysis is not sufficiently detailed in the context of the client's case, eg the candidate demonstrates little or no understanding of the key issues and risks; fails to apply the law to the facts to reach reasonable conclusions
Identify any ethical and professional conduct issues and exercise judgement to resolve them honestly and with integrity	• Where relevant, the candidate recognises ethical issues and exercises effective judgement in addressing them in accordance with the SRA Principles and rules of professional conduct	• The candidate does not recognise ethical issues or exercise effective judgement in addressing them in accordance with the SRA Principles and rules of professional conduct

PERFORMANCE INDICATORS FOR SQE2 LEGAL RESEARCH ASSESSMENT CRITERIA

Skills	*Indicators demonstrating competence*	*Indicators that do not demonstrate competence*
Identify and use relevant sources and information	• The candidate selects relevant information about the legal issue, or the client's problem, from the primary and/or secondary sources provided, eg o the candidate identifies relevant legislation/cases and/or legal explanations/commentary in a practitioner's text, or legal encyclopaedia o the candidate extracts relevant material, such as particular provision(s) from a statute, or legal rule(s) from the Civil Procedure Rules • The candidate uses their findings to substantiate/support their answer to the question(s) asked	• The candidate selects only irrelevant information from the primary and/or secondary sources provided • The candidate selects insufficient relevant information from the primary and/or secondary sources provided • The candidate is unable to distinguish between information that is relevant to the legal issue or the client's problem, and information that is irrelevant, eg the candidate's answer contains information drawn from all sources regardless of relevance, or from a number of irrelevant sources • The candidate does not use their findings to substantiate/support the answer to the question(s) asked
Provide advice which is client-focused and addresses the client's problem	• The candidate demonstrates an understanding of the client's problem from the client's perspective, eg the candidate addresses the client's legal problem, any relevant commercial considerations and/or the client's priorities, objectives and constraints	• The candidate does not understand the problem from the client's perspective, eg they focus on irrelevant issues/provide advice that does not take into account the client's priorities, objectives or constraints, or is inappropriate for the client's situation
Use clear, precise, concise and acceptable language	• The candidate uses understandable and simple language to convey facts and information effectively • The candidate uses correct legal terminology where necessary	• The reader struggles to understand the candidate's use of language; the answer lacks clarity and/or is poorly expressed • The reader's understanding is adversely affected by the density or brevity of the answer • The candidate uses unnecessary or confusing technical terms/legal jargon

Law	*Indicators demonstrating competence*	*Indicators that do not demonstrate competence*
Apply the law correctly to the client's situation	• The candidate identifies the relevant legal principles and applies them correctly to the facts of the client's case	• The candidate does not identify and apply the correct legal principles to the facts of the client's case • The candidate identifies the correct legal principles but misapplies them to the client's case
Apply the law comprehensively to the client's situation	• The candidate's legal analysis is sufficiently detailed in the context of the facts of the case, eg the candidate draws on multiple sources of information to address the legal issue/client's problem effectively	• The candidate's legal analysis is not sufficiently detailed in the context of the facts of the client's case
Identify any ethical and professional conduct issues and exercise judgement to resolve them honestly and with integrity	• Where relevant, the candidate recognises ethical issues and exercises effective judgement in addressing them in accordance with the SRA Principles and rules of professional conduct	• The candidate does not recognise ethical issues or exercise effective judgement in addressing them in accordance with the SRA Principles and rules of professional conduct

PERFORMANCE INDICATORS FOR SQE2 LEGAL WRITING ASSESSMENT CRITERIA

Skills	*Indicators demonstrating competence*	*Indicators that do not demonstrate competence*
Include relevant facts	• The candidate refers to and/or addresses the salient facts provided in their instructions. Salient facts could include facts that are important in ensuring the client's needs/objectives are met, or relevant to legal advice	• The candidate includes many facts in their answer that have no bearing on their legal advice
Use a logical structure	• The candidate's presentation of information is well organised, set out clearly and easy to follow • The reader is able to understand the candidate's answer without difficulty	• The candidate's presentation of information is confused and rambling • The reader is unable to follow or understand the candidate's answer
Advice/content is client- and recipient-focused	• The candidate demonstrates an understanding of the client's circumstances including their needs, objectives and priorities • The candidate, where relevant and appropriate, explores options and advises on strategies and solutions • The candidate takes into account who the client is; recognises the key issues in the case and considers any risks • Where appropriate, the candidate imparts any difficult or unwelcome news clearly and sensitively	• The candidate does not understand the client's perspective, eg they focus on irrelevant issues/provide extraneous advice/fail to advise on relevant options, strategies and solutions • The candidate fails to take into account who the client is and does not recognise the key issues in the case or consider any risks • The candidate lacks empathy or sensitivity if imparting difficult or unwelcome news
Use clear, precise, concise and acceptable language which is appropriate to the recipient	• The reader understands the candidate's use of language and clarity of expression • The candidate's language is appropriate to the recipient and the situation • The candidate avoids unnecessary technical terms/legal jargon • The candidate uses formalities appropriate to the context and purpose of the communication	• The reader struggles to understand the candidate's use of language; the answer lacks clarity and/or is poorly expressed • The reader's understanding is adversely affected by the density or brevity of the answer • The candidate uses language that is not appropriate to the recipient and/or the situation, eg the candidate adopts an essay-style approach • The candidate uses unnecessary or confusing technical terms/legal jargon

Law	*Indicators demonstrating competence*	*Indicators that do not demonstrate competence*
Apply the law correctly to the client's situation	• The candidate identifies the correct legal principles and applies them correctly to the facts of the case	• The candidate does not identify the correct legal principles • The candidate does not apply the legal principles correctly to the client's situation
Apply the law comprehensively to the client's situation	• The candidate's writing is of sufficient detail in the context of the client's situation and the relevant factual and legal issues	• The candidate's writing is not sufficiently detailed in the context of the client's situation and the relevant factual and legal issues
Identify any ethical and professional conduct issues and exercise judgement to resolve them honestly and with integrity	• Where relevant, the candidate recognises ethical issues and exercises effective judgement in addressing them in accordance with the SRA Principles and rules of professional conduct	• The candidate does not recognise ethical issues or exercise effective judgement in addressing them in accordance with the SRA Principles and rules of professional conduct

PERFORMANCE INDICATORS FOR SQE2 LEGAL DRAFTING ASSESSMENT CRITERIA

Skills	*Indicators demonstrating competence*	*Indicators that do not demonstrate competence*
Use clear, precise, concise and acceptable language	• The candidate uses understandable and simple language to convey facts and information effectively • The candidate uses words and phrases that are suitably formal for the document being drafted • The candidate uses correct legal terminology where necessary • The document uses as few words as possible without compromising the quality of the answer	• The candidate's answer is consistently wordy, repetitive or confusing and cannot be easily understood • The meaning of the document cannot be ascertained because it contains few words • The candidate uses inappropriate language, eg the language is too informal or casual • The candidate uses unnecessary technical terms/ legal jargon throughout
Structure the document appropriately and logically	• The candidate presents facts and information in a methodical way, eg the focus, flow and direction of each paragraph is clear and appropriate signposts are used to guide the reader through the document • The way in which the candidate sets out the contents of the document achieve its purpose	• The candidate's arrangement of facts or information is disjointed or confusing, eg the paragraphing or sequencing of information is illogical • The way in which the candidate sets out the contents of the document does not achieve its purpose
Law	*Indicators demonstrating competence*	*Indicators that do not demonstrate competence*
Draft a document which is legally correct	• The candidate identifies the correct legal principles in accordance with the SQE2 assessment specification and applies them correctly in their drafting • The candidate's drafting is legally effective, eg the document contains all key information or the names of relevant parties	• The candidate does not identify the correct legal principles • The candidate does not apply the legal principles correctly in their drafting • The candidate's drafting is not legally effective
Draft a document which is legally comprehensive	• The candidate's drafting is sufficiently detailed in the context of the client's situation and the relevant factual and legal issues	• The candidate's drafting is not sufficiently detailed in the context of the client's situation and the relevant factual and legal issues
Identify any ethical and professional conduct issues and exercise judgement to resolve them honestly and with integrity	• Where relevant, the candidate recognises ethical issues and exercises effective judgement in addressing them in accordance with the SRA Principles and rules of professional conduct	• The candidate does not recognise ethical issues or exercise effective judgement in addressing them in accordance with the SRA Principles and rules of professional conduct